1

Copyright Notice

Strolling Around Siena by Irene Reid

ISBN: 9781977012524

Book Cover

Photo by Irene Reid

Enhanced by Prisma Photo Editor

Get Ready

Torre del Mangia

If you want to climb the Torre del Mangia, you should aim to be in the Piazza del Campo early enough to give yourself a little time to look around the square before joining the Tower ticket queue. Opening Times can be found here:

https://www.comune.siena.it/node/509

Note, they only let so many visitors up the tower at a time, and they sell a maximum of 950 tickets a day. If you plan to visit the adjoining Palazzo Pubblico as well, buy your ticket at the same time for the best deal.

Cathedral Complex

You need tickets to get into the Cathedral, the Baptistery, the Crypt and the Cathedral Museum. It's worth looking at the Opa pass which will save you 50% and lets you see sights not open to everyone. You can even hire a tablet to guide you round the highlights. Take a look at this web page:

https://operaduomo.siena.it/en/visit/

One of the highlights of the cathedral is its wonderful marble pavement, see page 108. If you would like to see all of it, you need to visit in September when its protective covering is lifted for a few weeks.

Palazzo Chigi-Saracini

You will see this palace, which is now the Music Academy, at the end of Walk 3. Its interior is very beautiful so you could consider a tour but you need to pre-book. The best plan is to check at the tourist office as soon as you arrive.

Another possibility is attending a concert which again you would need to pre-book. The schedule can be found here:

https://www.chigiana.org/concerti/

Potted History

According to legend Siena was founded by Senius and Aschius. They were the sons of Remus who fled Rome after Dad was murdered by Uncle Romulus.

Siena holds onto this link with ancient Rome, and you will see many statues of the famous She-Wolf who suckled Romulus and Remus. Perhaps this Roman link is true but there is no proof. What we do know is that the Romans built Siena Julia as a military outpost when Augustus was Caesar. Its hill-top position made it very defensible.

Siena then grew into a successful trading post and pottered along until it suddenly expanded in the 6th century AD. That happened because the Lombards and then the Franks (both conquering Germanic tribes) took over northern Italy, and between them they constructed a major road from Rome to France, the Via Francigena. Siena lay right on it – what an opportunity for trade and travel! Boom time!

This put Siena in direct competition with its neighbour Florence. The two towns were in constant economic and military competition as they fought for supremacy and territory. Also, politically Florence supported the Pope (Guelphs), whereas Siena supported the monarchy (Ghibellines). The two towns were never going to be friendly neighbours!

However, despite this unpleasant background, Siena bloomed and artists of all types flocked to the city and adorned it with beautiful monuments and buildings.

4

The Nine

In 1287 the Republic of Siena was ruled by The Council of Nine, a well-intentioned governing body that instigated many worthwhile and much loved improvements which you can still see today.

Siena barred members of the wealthiest and most powerful families from joining the Council of Nine, because the temptation to govern for their personal gain was seen as being far too strong.

The Twelve

As you might expect that restriction on who could govern and who couldn't didn't go down well with everyone. In 1355 Charles VI and the richest families in Siena ousted The Council of Nine and put The Government of the Twelve in its place. It consisted of six members from the noble families and six from the merchant families.

The Black Death

During all this political upheaval, Siena also had to deal with The Black Death which devastated Siena in 1348. Over several months it killed about 60% of the population. Siena had little option other than to dig huge deep pits all around the city where the citizens could drop the dead. Every day for several months, workers would throw soil on top of the bodies ready for the next day's arrivals. The Black Death was of course Bubonic plague. Incredibly Siena's population did not recover in numbers until the twentieth century.

Drought and Famine also hit Siena during this time which let to riots and rebellions.

Florence Takeover

Siena never really got back on its feet and was finally defeated and taken over by Florence in 1555. Peace brought prosperity to Siena once again, even as a satellite of Florence.

Earthquake

This part of Tuscany was hit by a powerful earthquake in 1798. It caused tremendous damage to many of the buildings in Siena, but Siena did rebuild and recover.

Italian at Last

Italy only became a united country in the nineteenth century, after battling with Austria and Spain to gain independence. So when Italy finally formed a republic, Siena became part of the region of Tuscany.

The Maps

There are maps sprinkled all through the walks to help you find your way. If you need to check where you are at any point during a walk, always flip back to find the map you need.

To help you follow the maps, each map shows its start point. In addition numbered directions have been placed on each map. The numbers correspond to the directions within the walks.

The Walks

Walk 1 - The Campo

Takes you around the sights of the the Piazza del Campo, Siena's heart.

Walk 2 - Siena North (2.7km)

Takes you north of the Campo and outside the wall. You can see some churches, ancient fountains, and visit one of Siena's important museums.

Walk 3 - To the Cathedral and back (2.5km or 2.3km)

Takes you to the four most important religious buildings in Siena, The Santa Caterina Sanctuary, the Basilica San Domenico, the Baptistery, and the Cathedral.

Walk 4 – Siena South (1.4km or 2.0 km)

Takes you around some more contradas before arriving in Market Square and the old ghetto area.

Tip

Ideally you will have enough time to follow all the above walks and really stroll around. However if you arrive in Siena on a day trip, your time will be very limited, so your best plan is to follow Walk 1 and then Walk 3. This will include most of the most famous sights and will easily fill your day.

Movie Locations

For movie buffs, Siena appears in the James Bond movie Quantum of Solace, and the walks will point these out as you reach them.

Foods to Try

Panforte di Siena

When you stop for a coffee, try to include a slice of Panforte di Siena.

It's a traditional fruit cake from the thirteenth century, filled with nuts, spices, fruits and bound together with butter and sugar. The locals eat it mainly at Christmas with a coffee or a dessert wine.

It has played its part in Siena's turbulent past. In 1260 Siena fought a crucial battle with Florence at Montaperti. It's said that one of the reasons Siena won that vital battle, was the rich bread filled with fruit and nuts which the soldiers ate – the original Panforte. It filled the soldiers with energy compared to the Florentine soldiers who had far poorer provisions

Pici alle briciole

This is a very simple spaghetti-like pasta which is served with a sauce of garlic, olive oil, chilli, and breadcrumbs.

Ricciarelli di Siena

These are soft almond marzipan biscuits. The recipe was brought back to Siena from Arabia by Ricciardetto della Gheardesca when he returned from the Crusades.

In those days the ingredients were expensive, so these biscuits were only eaten by the very wealthy.

Walk 1 – The Campo

This walk starts at the most famous spot in Siena, the Piazza del Campo.

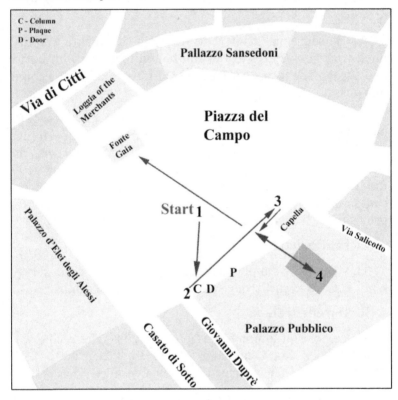

Map 1

Piazza del Campo

Many European countries claim to have the most beautiful square in the world, and this must be Italy's contender.

It started as a marketplace where the three hillside communities that coalesced to form Siena met.

The Piazza's pavement of red bricks explode out into a sunburst of nine strips of travertine, one for each member of the Council of Nine who ruled over the city at the height of its mediaeval splendour.

Eleven narrow shady streets give access to the rest of the city. The palaces that run round the square are very uniform. When they were built they had to follow the rule:

**One building will not stand out beyond another,
but they shall be disposed and arranged equally
so as to be of the greatest beauty for the city.**

The Contrade

Siena has 17 Contrade or city neighbourhoods, and each Contrada has its own flag, its own seat of government, its own constitution, its own church, fountain, hymn, motto, insignia, patron saint, and of course geographical boundaries. All this was established in 1729.

Every year, on a Contrada's Saint's Day, all the babies born during the year are baptized at the fountain of the Contrada. The baby is given a fazzoletto (a scarf) and a certificate as it joins the Contrada for life. The Contrada will be part of the child's life forever, through good times and bad, and at all of the great moments in life as well as the little ones. They are family.

You will stroll through several Contrade on this walk.

The Palio

This is the famous horse race that is held in the Campo twice each year, on July 2 and August 16.

When the Grand Duke of Tuscany outlawed bullfighting, the competitive Contrade took to organizing races in the Piazza del Campo. The first races were on buffalos, then donkeys, and finally the Palio, that terrifying horse race. They race for a simple trophy, a painted banner bearing the image of the

Virgin Mary. They ride bareback, are dressed in the appropriate colours, and a magnificent pageant precedes the race. It attracts visitors and spectators from around the world.

The field consists of only ten horses for safety reasons, so not all seventeen Contrade can take part in every race. The seven Contrade that did not take part in the previous race are automatically included; and three more are chosen by a raffle.

Each Contrada is assigned a racehorse from the pool of Palio horses, just days before the race, so there is a lot of luck on which Contrada gets a good horse.

The start of the Palio is quite different from other horse-races. The starting official, who decides the position of each horse on the start-line, can only do so just before the scheduled start. The race actually starts once the 10th horse reaches its position – and just to make it even more exciting that rider must gallop to the start line. Once he crosses the start line the other nine riders can set off. The start of the race is tactical, as the 10th rider can choose his moment to start galloping. The tension before the race finally begins, climbs and climbs.

As you can imagine the horses don't stand in an orderly line during all that waiting. They move about and the result is that when the starting rider finally goes for it, some of the horses may be out of position, resulting in many false starts before the race really gets going.

The race circles the Piazza del Campo three times and usually lasts no more than 90 seconds. The Palio differs from "normal" horse races in that part of the game is to prevent rival Contrade from winning. When a Contrada fails to win, its historical enemy will celebrate that fact nearly as merrily as a victory of its own.

Few things are forbidden to the jockeys during the race; for instance, they can pull or shove their fellow riders, hit the horses and each other, or try to hamper other horses at the start. The riders are allowed to use whips, and are allowed to whip the other horses. The winner is the first horse across the line, with or without a rider.

It is not uncommon for a few of the jockeys to be thrown off their horses while making the treacherous turns in the piazza, so it's not unusual to see horses finishing the race riderless.

It's quite a spectacle.

Nonna

A long-standing tradition of the Palio is that the Contrada which has the longest stretch without a win is nicknamed Nonna, which means granny.

Pressure mounts on the Nonna Contrada every year, until they finally win and pass the dreaded nickname to another Contrada. At the time of writing the Wolf Contrada is Nonna.

Stand in front of the Palazzo Pubblico

Palazzo Pubblico

The Palazzo Pubblico, which dominates the square, was the seat of government in Siena and where the Council of Nine sat.

The Nine were dedicated to the welfare and administration of the city. Amazingly once elected, the Nine were actually confined to the Palace and only permitted to leave on feast days!

Standing in front of the palace, you can see that the whole building curves slightly to fit the curve of the Campo. Its impressive tower was purposely built to be taller than any tower in Florence, Siena's great rival. In fact at the time it went up, it was the tallest tower in Italy. The architect also ensured it was just as tall as Siena Cathedral – to make the point that church and state were equal in Siena.

She-Wolf Gargoyles

Look right to the top of the tower and you will see eight gargoyles leaning out, two at each of the four corners – however they are not the usual gruesome gargoyles, but instead they portray the legendary she-wolf.

San Bernardino

The distinctive stone disc in the centre of the façade contains a San Bernardino monogram – it's a sun holding the letters IHS which represents the name Jesus in Greek.

San Bernardino came from Siena but he travelled all over Italy, preaching sermons to try to stop the various cities warring against each other – including here in the Piazza del Campo. His sermons were legendary and lasted all day.

San Bernardino encouraged the warring Guelphs and Ghibellines to replace their own banners and logos with the San Bernardino Monogram as a peaceful action. He died in the city of L'Aquila and legend says that blood appeared on his grave until the warring factions in that city made peace.

He later became the patron saint of advertisers because of his great powers of persuasion.

Medici Coat of Arms

Further down in the middle of the façade is the Medici coat of arms with a crown on top. The Medici family were the rulers of Florence who eventually conquered Siena - in fact they ruled most of Tuscany.

Map 1.1 - Face the Palazzo and walk diagonally right to reach the right-hand door of the palace.

She Wolves

Look above the door. You will spot a lion rampant, but more interestingly another two she-wolves suckling the brothers – the wolves look very much in need of a meal.

Very close to the door stands a column topped with yet another she-wolf.

Map 1.2 – Walk along the front of the Palazzo Pubblico. You will reach a little chapel which protrudes from the front of the Palazzo and sits at the foot of the tower.

Capella di Piazza

This little chapel was built to celebrate the end of the plague which brought such devastation to Siena. The figures standing in the niches are six of the twelve apostles – they planned to have all twelve but the money ran out.

Towering above you is the Torre del Mangia

Torre del Mangia

The tower can be seen from all Siena, so if you get lost you can use it as a guide.

It was built in the fourteenth century. Legend has it that that at the 4 corners of the tower there are stones which have Latin and Hebrew engraved on them, and that they have the power to ward off gales and thunderstorms.

The stones' power ran out in the fifteenth century when the tower was hit by lightning. The original plan was to have two towers, but the funds for the second tower had to be diverted to restore the tower you see now.

Old Joe

The tower's striking style has been copied by other cities, including Old Joe at the University of Birmingham England.

Map 1.3 – Now go into the Palazzo courtyard – the door is just to the right of the little chapel.

The Courtyard

The Tower's name means Tower of the Eater and refers to its first guardian, Giovanni di Balduccio, who was a glutton and reputedly spent all his money on food. You will see a very weathered statue of "the glutton" in the arched courtyard.

Spot another "she-wolf" statue at the back of the courtyard.

Now stand in the middle of the courtyard and look up to see the tower high above you. There is no elevator and the climb is more than 500 steps.

You will find the ticket-office in the courtyard for tickets to climb the tower and/or visit the Palazzo museum.

If you don't want to climb the tower, skip to "Visiting the Museum" on page 20.

Climbing the Tower

It's quite a climb to the top, but it's worthwhile as the views over the town and Tuscany are wonderful – so get climbing.

When you reach the top you can enjoy wonderful views of Siena. Spot the cathedral with its black and white tower in the distance, and enjoy the expanse of red-roofed buildings of the old town.

Sunto

Look up to see Sunto, the largest bell in the tower weighing in at over six tons. It was put up there in 1666 and it is rung on just one occasion – when a Palio is about to be run.

The Italian Poet Eugenio Montale (a Nobel Prize Winner) wrote about Sunto in 1939

> A bronze sound falls from the tower:
> the parade continues between drums that beat back
> to the glory of the districts
> and the amazement that invades the shell of the Campo

The name Sunto is short for Assunta as it is dedicated to the Madonna dell'Assunta. The Assumption is the moment when the Virgin Mary ascends to heaven.

When you are ready to move on, carefully descend back to the courtyard.

Visiting the Museum

If you don't want to visit the museum, continue the walk from "Exiting the Tower" on page 26.

If you don't want to visit the museum, continue the walk from "Exiting the Tower" on page 26.

The Museum

Nearly every major room in the Palazzo contains very colourful frescoes, unusually commissioned by the government rather than by the Church.

Sala di Balia

The colourful frescoes in this room celebrate Pope Alexander III, who came from Siena.

His papal career was a difficult one. When his predecessor died, there followed a long and torturous dispute over who was the next Pope. The rivals were Alexander III and Victor IV.

Alexander III was either in residence in Rome or in exile, depending on how much support he had from the crowns of Europe at any time. He was even exiled to Venice at one point when his rival Victor IV took the papal throne.

Alexander's main problem in securing the papal crown was Barbarossa, the German Holy Roman Emperor. Barbarossa

20

was only willing to accept Alexander as Pope if Alexander submitted to his authority – and Alexander was having none of that. It was not until Barbarossa was heavily defeated in battle that he conceded defeat and finally accepted Alexander III as pope.

This room celebrates Alexander's life and his conflict with Barbarossa. It shows his exile to Venice and his return to Rome accompanied by Barbarossa.

The Battle of Punta San Salvatore
One of the most interesting frescoes is "The Battle of Punta San Salvatore" which sits over one of the doorways.

It shows a very exciting battle scene between the German and Venetian armadas.

If you look closely you can see the Lion of St Mark on the Venetian shields and the German Eagle on the German shields. Venice is shown as winning the battle since they were supporters of Pope Alexander.

Interestingly this battle is thought to have never actually taken place, so you could say this was a very early example of Fake News.

Sala del Risorgimento

This room was redecorated after the death of Italy's first king, Vittorio Emmanuelle II. It celebrates his life, the battles for independence from Austria and Spain who ruled vast parts of what is now Italy, and the final unification of Italy.

Sala dei Nove

In this room you can see an interesting set of frescoes called the Effects of Good and Bad Government by Ambrogio Lorenzetti.

Allegory of Good Government

On the smaller wall opposite the windows, you will see an Allegory of Good Government.

It's a kind of medieval government information poster. It sounds a bit of a yawn but it is interesting if you compare the fresco's message to most governments of the time.

The chap on the throne represents Siena and embodies Good Government. The little children at his feet are of course Romulus and Remus and the wolf.

The ladies on either side of the throne represent Peace, Fortitude, and Prudence on the left, with Magnanimity,

22

Temperance and Justice on the right. Peace is the lady furthest left who seems very relaxed and laid back.

On the far left we see Justice balancing the scales.

Below are two groups of men. Those on the right are in chains and might be prisoners from Florence. Those on the left are the founding fathers of the city.

The Effect of Good Government

Just to drive the point home, we see "The Effect of Good Government" on the longer wall of the room, showing everyone having a great time.

You can see a school full of happy children, busy shops, and farmers bringing in the harvest.

The nine ladies at the centre of the fresco are thought to be the nine Muses, who symbolise beauty and justice.

Now take a look at Bad Government, which is in much poorer condition.

This time Tyranny, complete with horns and fangs, sits on the throne and stares back at us. He is accompanied by Avarice, Pride, Vanity, Cruelty, Treason, Fraud, Frenzy, and War. On the floor in front of Tyranny lies Justice with her shattered scales lying around her.

Finally we see "The Effect of Bad Government" where the countryside is barren and no one is cultivating the land. Robbers and thugs roam the streets, homes are ablaze, and Siena is in a sorry state.

The entire fresco cycle shows how seriously the Sienese considered the government of their city and it's impressive for that fact alone.

Sala del **Mappamondo** (Hall of the Globe)

You probably expected a globe of the world when you walked in! There was indeed once a wooden rotating map of Siena's territory. However it has been lost and we are left with just the room name.

The golden "Majesty" by Martini which is on the left wall survived. It is one of the highlights of the museum. You see the Virgin Mary surrounded by various saints and apostles, all seated under a colourful canopy.

Mary is discussing Siena with the assembled saints, and her thoughts were written on the painting. Only two speeches have survived to today.

The first is a blessing to all citizens, except anyone who victimises the weak. The second is a warning to anyone who looks after their own interests over that of Siena.

Guidoriccio da Fogliano - Simone Martini

Also worth a look is the fresco of Guidoriccio, a mercenary who commanded the Sienese army as they conquered the castles of Montemassi and Sassoforte. The castle on the left is Montemassi, and behind Guidoriccio is an army camp full of soldiers ready to attack.

Guidoriccio and his warhorse are depicted in very dapper matching outfits - his warhorse was killed in the battle of Montemassi.

Blessed Beato Sansedoni

When you get back to the Piazza del Campo you will see the Palazzo Sansedoni. So take a look at the painting of Beato Sansedoni which is in this room. He is protectively holding the city of Siena.

Exiting the Tower

Map 1.4 – Exit the Palazzo.

With the Palazzo entrance behind you, walk straight ahead to reach the fountain on the opposite side of the square.

Fonte Gaia

As you wander around Siena you will soon realise that water is a very series business – how could it be otherwise in a city perched on a hill.

The Sienese solved the problem of getting water up the hill with a maze of tunnels and hydraulics to drive the water to the fountains. They are hidden beneath your feet.

The tunnels were dug in the thirteenth century and it was dangerous work as they were prone to collapsing as they were excavated. However no-one was ever in danger of drowning as the precious water the tunnels carried was never more than a few inches deep! Ever since the tunnels were built, Siena has fought a constant battle to keep them open, functioning, and carrying clean water.

The Fonte Gaia is a rectangular basin encircled with ornate statuary. When they were added in 1419 they included the first female nudes on public view for centuries. They were later deemed far too shocking for the nineteenth-century city fathers. So two of the original nude statues were replaced with more modest versions

The fountain also hosts some wolves celebrating Siena's supposed origin from Rome. All the original statues are now in a museum which you can visit on Walk 3

Clean fresh precious water gushed from this fountain for the first time in 1346, and the Fountain of Joy was christened because of the sheer joy of the population.

In the eighteenth century one of the beautiful statues was broken when an over-enthusiastic fan climbed up the fountain to get a better view of the Palio – he was killed in the accident.

More recently, the Fountain and the Palio made an appearance in the James Bond film, Quantum of Solace, where Bond is seen emerging from the underground water tunnels at the Fonte Gaia as the Palio thunders by.

River Diana

There is a very old legend in Siena about the river Diana which is said to run under Siena. The experts think the legend is inspired by an ancient underground Roman aqueduct which disappeared when the Roman Empire fell, but since then the thirsty people of Siena have searched for this legendary river.

Some claim to have heard the water flowing beneath their feet but it's never been found. The department which today takes care of Siena's tunnels and water supply has adopted the name "Diana", and I am sure they are keeping a keen eye out for any trace of the river.

Palazzo Sansedoni

With your back to the town hall, look to the right of the fountain and you will see a very handsome red palace with a tower at the curve of the Campo.

Palazzo Sansedoni.

It was the home of one of Siena's most aristocratic families from the Middle Ages. Their most famous member was Beato Sansedoni who was a very religious man, a great orator, and a politician – you might have seen the painting of him inside the Palazzo Pubblico.

When he died, Siena put a bust of him on the façade of the Cathedral, and even ran a Palio to commemorate his name. Inside the palace there is a beautiful chapel dedicated to Beato, and city authorities attend mass there once a year to mark the day he died.

Face the fountain again and turn left to see the castle-like Palazzo d'Elci degli Alessi.

Palazzo d'Elci degli Alessi

Again this was built by a wealthy family. More interestingly, the Palio start and finish line which is called The Mossa, sits just below it. So the windows of this Palace are probably the best viewing spot in the square.

Stand facing the fountain with the Palazzo Pubblico behind you.

You can proceed with any of Walks 2, 3, or 4 from this point.

Walk 2 – Siena North

This walk starts in the Piazza del Campo.

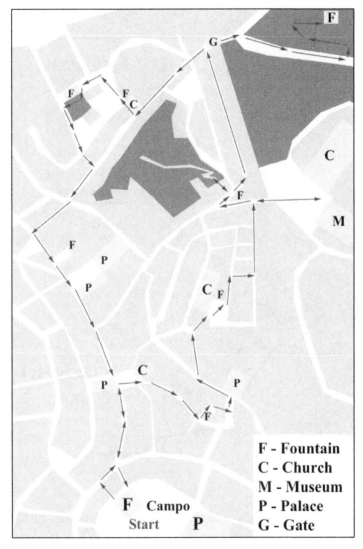

Walk 2 Overview

It will take you to the Contrada of the Owl, the Giraffe, The Caterpillar, and the Wolf.

You will visit churches, an art museum, and see some palaces and fountains.

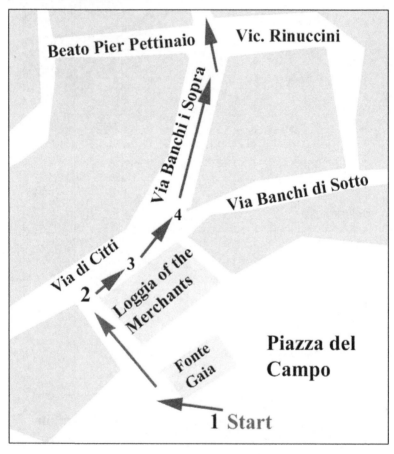

Map 2

Map 2.1 - Face the Fonte Gaia with the Palazzo Pubblico behind you.

Look behind the fountain and you will see two archways, one on each side of the fountain. Leave the square by the left-hand archway.

Some stairs will take you up onto Via di Citti which is the main thoroughfare of Siena.

Map 2.2 - Turn right and on your right-hand side is the columned Loggia of the Merchants

Loggia of the Merchants

The pillars of the Loggia are adorned with statues of Saint Peter and Saint Paul, and three patron saints of Siena, Saint Savino, Saint Ansano and Saint Vittore.

In the loggia you can see two ornate stone benches, as well as a striking colourful ceiling and floor. Unfortunately you will have to look through the iron gates to see the details, as at the time of writing there is no public access.

The Loggia was built in the fifteenth century and was the meeting place of Siena's merchants and money lenders. It was here that deals were made and fortunes won and lost – it also gave the merchants some shelter from the hot Italian sun.

Map 2.3 - Continue walking in the same direction and you will come to a fork in the road.

Croce del Travaglio

This was once known as Croce del Travaglio, and it is where you find the intersection of the original three main thoroughfares of Siena, Via Banchi di Sopra, Via Banchi di Sotto, and Via di Città.

Map 2.4 - Take the left hand road. Follow Via Banchi di Sopra uphill, passing Vicolo Rinuccini on your right, and Vicolo Beato Pier Pettinaio on your left.

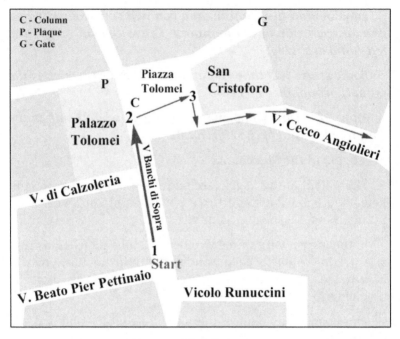

C - Column
P - Plaque
G - Gate

Map 3

***Map 3.1 - Continue straight ahead along Banchi di Sopra.
You will pass Vicolo del Coltellinaio on your left and then
reach Piazza Tolomei.***

Contrada of the Owl and Piazza Tolomei

This is the centre of Siena's smallest district, and
traditionally its residents were bankers. Their symbol is a
crowned owl sitting on a branch, and their motto is:

I see in the night

It is believed that a temple to Minerva, the roman goddess
of wisdom, once stood in this area and held a statue of Minerva
with an owl in her hands.

The owl is also a symbol for envy in Italy and the hooting
owl is supposed to be claiming, "All mine! All mine!" – In

34

Italian of course. Many of Siena's banks were once located here so the greedy association seems appropriate.

The Owl Contrada was Nonna for 30 years. But their luck finally changed in 2009.

Behind this piazza once lay Siena's red light district, full of bars and brothels – but they are all gone now!

The piazza welcomes you with another column topped with the she-wolf and Romulus and Remus. The she-wolf faces the pretty Palazzo Tolomei - look up to see the palace's beautiful windows.

Palazzo Tolomei

It is one of the oldest palaces in Siena, and was built in the thirteenth century for one of Siena's powerful and wealthy families, the Tolomei.

Some claim that the Tolomei family can trace its origins back to the Ptolemaic dynasty of Egypt whose most famous member was of course Cleopatra.

Tolomei and Salvani feud

The Tolomei family made a fortune in banking in the twelfth century. Their family history illustrates the deep division in Italy between the Guelph and the Ghibelline factions.

The Tolomeis were a Guelph family and because of that they were exiled from Siena in 1267, as Siena was a Ghibelline city.

Their arch enemies, the Salvani family, took their chance and wrecked the Palazzo of their hated neighbours in their absence.

The Tolomeis returned to Sienna after the Guelph victory in 1269. They rebuilt their palace from the stone and pillars of the Salvani palace which in its turn had been destroyed.

Despite various mishaps over the centuries the Piazza Tolomei has survived to this day.

The palace also has a literary connection. Pia dei Tolomei was born here, she stars in one of the most tragic stories in Dante's Divine Comedy:

Remember me, the one who is Pia;
Siena made me, Maremma undid me:
he knows it, the one who first encircled
my finger with his jewel, when he married me.

The story tells us how Pia was married off to the lord of Maremma, and ended up being thrown from a tower window to her death.

There is a plaque commemorating this verse nearby. Face the palazzo and go round its right hand side to find it on the wall. Then return to the square.

Map 3.2 - Behind the she-wolf stands the church of Saint Christopher so walk over to reach it.

San Cristoforo

It is one of the oldest in Sienna and is also the church of the Owl Contrada.

> Before the Palazzo Pubblico was built on the Campo, the town's ruling body met in this church to legislate and run Siena.
>
> It was in this church that Siena declared war on Florence in 1260. A deputation from Florence arrived to demand that Siena open its city walls, and informed Siena that Florence would be installing commanders to rule the city.
>
> The Council of Twelve met in this church and realised war with Florence was inevitable. They desperately needed to hire a German mercenary army to have any chance of defeating Florence, but mercenaries were expensive and Siena didn't have the funds.
>
> Salmimbene Salimbeni who was the founder of the city's first bank, the Monte dei Paschi, marched home and filled a wheelbarrow with gold florins which he gave to the council to fund the battle. Siena won the vital battle of Montaperti which resulted in 10,000 deaths.

The church was badly damaged in the 1798 earthquake and was more or less rebuilt. It got a new-style façade as part of that reconstruction, and it was financed by the Tolomei family.

Perhaps that explains why the church door is guarded by two statues of members of the Tolomei family, Saint Bernardo Tolomei, and the Blessed Nera Tolomei.

If it's open pop in for a quick look around. Most of the best art is now in one of Siena's museums.

The church does have a cloister but you have to exit the church and turn right to go round the side to reach an archway and the entrance gate – and it will probably be locked. If you have time have a quick look just in case it's open, then return to the church door.

Map 3.3 - Face the church door and leave the square by the right hand side of the church.

Follow Via Cecco Angiolieri downhill to reach Vicolo del Vento on your left

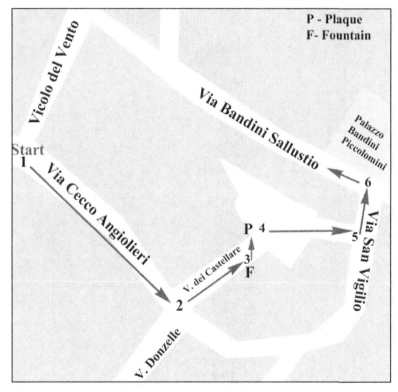

Map 4

Map 4.1 – Continue downhill on Via Cecco Angiolieri to find the archway which leads to little Vicolo dei Castellare.

It's on your left and just before the more obvious Vicolo Donzelle on the right.

Map 4.2 - Go through the archway and a few steps will bring you to the Owl fountain on your right.

The Owl Fountain

The Owl Fountain

It depicts an owl in flight on top of a tall pole, but you must stand in just the right spot to see it at its best.

You might wonder where the water is! Well it's a very discrete fountain, and when needed the water flows down the column the owl is standing on.

Map 4.3 - Follow this little street to walk into a courtyard. This was the centre of the medieval Ugurgieri family castle.

Castellare degli Ugurgieri

Important Sienese families all used to live in fortified structures similar to this one, but this is the only one to survive. The Ugurgieri were wealthy landowners and part of the Owl contrada. Today the castle complex houses the Owl Contrada's headquarters.

The Contrada put up a wall plaque in this courtyard just last century in honour of Giovanni Ugurgieri, who led his men to victory in the battle of Montaperto against Florence. It's said that the spirit of Giovanni Ugurgieri, who died in that battle, still haunts this courtyard.

You can see the plaque on the left hand side of the courtyard as you enter.

Translating the plaque:

> **The people of the Priora Contrada of the Civetta have chosen this "Castellare" as its Oratory and Seat in remembrance of Giovanni Ugurgieri who brought glory to this territory after leading his men and Siena to victory at Montaperti and whose heroic image still lives 700 years later**

Montaperto was the famous battle against Siena's eternal rival Florence which you read about at San Cristoforo.

Florence's army was encamped not far from town and Siena's leaders were locked in a furious debate on the emergency. The desperate townspeople marched to the Cathedral where they were joined by the clergy. Together they stood before the altar and pledged themselves and Siena to the Virgin Mary if she would give them victory.

The legend then tells us that the Virgin sent snow which hid the Sienese army, and led to their victory against all the odds. It's reckoned that Florence and the Guelphs lost 10,000 men on that day.

From that day on Siena thought of itself as favoured by the Virgin Mary – that is one of the reasons why the Palio prize is a banner with the Virgin Mary on it.

Map 4.4 - Follow the path through the courtyard to exit by a second archway.

Map 4.5 – Turn left along Via San Vigilio. You will reach a T-junction with Via Sallustio Bandini.

In front of you is the Palazzo Bandini-Piccolomini.

Palazzo Bandini-Piccolomini

It was here that the priest and economist Sallustio Bandini was born. His father was from the Bandini family and he married Caterina Piccolomini – hence the palace's double-barrelled name. You will read more about Sallustio Bandini soon.

Take a look at the door to see some children riding dolphins. Above them is the shield of the Piccolomini family with its five crescent moons.

The iron rings you see lining the facade were used to tether visitors' horses.

At the time of writing the palace is owned by the University of Siena – although they are trying to sell it.

Map 4.6 – Facing the door, turn left to walk along Via Sallustio Bandini.

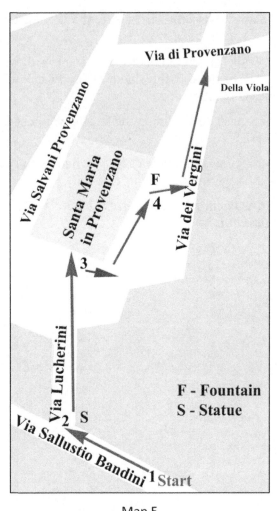

Map 5

Map 5.1 - Continue along Via Sallustio Bandini to the corner with Via Lucherini on your right.

Take a look at the little corner altar of the Madonna and Child. There are often flowers placed below it.

Map 5.2 – Turn right into Via Lucherini and walk downhill to reach the gleaming white church in front of you, Santa Maria in Provenzano.

Contrada of the Giraffe

You are now in Giraffe country. This is a Royal Contrada because it won the Palio in the presence of King Umberto I.

Traditionally, the Contrada's residents were painters, and its symbol is a giraffe led by a Moor. Their Royal title is commemorated by a legend beneath the giraffe:

Umbertus I dedit

Given by Umberto I

The contrada motto is "Higher is the head, greater is the glory" which seems appropriate for a giraffe.

Santa Maria in Provenzano

Legend has it that one of the houses on this square had a terracotta image of the Virgin Mary on the facade, which a passing Spaniard decided to shoot. The gun exploded in the process and so did the Spaniard.

The surviving head of the Madonna was immediately declared a miracle and this church went up to house it. When it was completed the whole town turned out to see the statue moved into its new abode.

Go in and walk down to the main altar where you can see the surviving piece of statuary surrounded by silver angels. At the bottom you will see two key Sienese religious figures; Saint Bernardino who you have already read about, and Saint Catherine who you will read about later.

The Rag

The prize for the July Palio is a hand painted silk banner known affectionately by the locals as The Rag. It is designed and painted anew every year to strict rules, and is kept in this church until one week before the race. Then there is a ceremony in the Palazzo Pubblico where The Rag is presented to the people, who examine it for any signs or omens as to who the winner will be.

The banner then returns to this church the night before the race, where it stands on display in candlelight along with the flags of every Contrada. Next day it is paraded in The Campo on a wagon pulled by four enormous oxen. Once the Palio is over, the winner returns the banner to the church, again as part of a grand procession, and sings a hymn of thanksgiving.

Map 5.3 - Once you exit the church, turn left to go round the church and down the stairs into little Piazzetta della Giraffa.

Piazzetta della Giraffa

This is where you will find the rather modern fountain of the giraffe. The animal at the front looks more like a horse really, but the animal in the background is definitely a giraffe.

Map 5.4 - Leave the little piazzetta by the sloping exit near the fountain.

Turn left along Via dei Vergini and pass Vicolo della Viola on your right. You will reach a crossroads with Via di Provenzano.

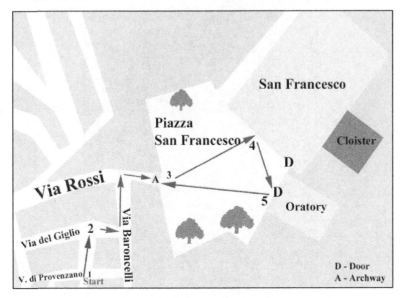

Map 6

Map 6.1 – Cross Via di Provenzano and walk along Via delle Vergini to reach a T junction with Via del Giglio.

Map 6.2 - Turn right into Via del Giglio. Then turn left into Via Baroncelli.

Finally turn right into Via Rossi and go under an archway to reach Piazza San Francesco.

48

Piazza San Francesco

You are now in the Contrada of the Caterpillar, and their symbol is a crowned caterpillar on a rose. Traditionally, the people of the Caterpillar worked in the silk trade and apparently have a reputation for being short tempered. Their motto is:

As revolution sounds my name

Map 6.3 - In front of you stands the Basilica of San Francesco. Walk towards it.

Basilica of San Francesco

The original Franciscan church caught fire in 1565 and was largely destroyed. So what you see now is the eighteenth century replacement

The Franciscan order believed in giving their wealth to the poor, therefore elaborate church decoration was frowned on. As a result the church is quite plain outside, other than the many coats of arms on the façade and a lovely rose window. The coats of arms honour the families who financed and maintained the church over the centuries.

Go inside if it's open.

49

Inside you will see that the church seems to be dressed in black and white striped pyjamas – a popular style in Tuscany.

Walk down the church and enjoy the light streaming through the stained glass windows.

Miracle of Siena

The Miracle of Siena occurred in this church.

In 1730, hundreds of consecrated hosts (the little wafers of bread used in communion) were stolen from the church along with the gold box they were stored in.

A few days later the hosts were discovered in the church poor box. The thief's conscience only went so far, as he did not return the gold box. The hosts were found to be undamaged, so the church declared them sacred and they were sealed away.

Over the centuries various popes have opened up the sealed box and declared the hosts still fresh and uncorrupted to this day.

The most intriguing investigation took place in 1914, when the Pope gave permission for the scientists to take a look.

They tested the hosts and how they were being stored, and concluded that they were indeed still edible and that there was no special storage method being used to keep them that way. Makes you think.

This church is supposedly the burial site of Pia dei Tolomei – the unfortunate lady you read about earlier in Dante's poem and who was thrown from a window.

The Cloister

The entrance to the cloister is about half-way down the nave on the right-hand side. If the door is closed, exit the basilica and turn left to make your way to an archway and door – it's another entrance to the cloister.

The cloister is peaceful and worth a visit. It is home to some statue fragments from the original church before the fire in 1565.

Exit the church/cloister to return to Piazza San Francesco.

Many of the old church buildings round the square are now part of the University of Siena.

Map 6.4 - Stand facing away from the church. You will find the entrance to the Oratory of San Bernardino on your left. It's the door with a blue circular panel high above it.

Oratory of San Bernardino

San Bernardino preached his fiery sermons in this square as well as on the Campo.

The blue circular panel represents the symbol which San Bernardino would often hold up to the crowd. It shows the rays of the sun with the monogram IHS in the middle – IHS comes from the first three letters of Jesus in Greek, ΙΗΣΟΥΣ. The monogram was often put over doorways all over Siena to ask for God's protection.

San Bernardino's Oratory now houses an art museum, the Museo Diocesano. The building itself is also quite beautiful, and a perfect setting for a collection of religious art.

Here are some favourites to spot if you decide to visit.

Saint George and the Dragon - Sano di Pietro

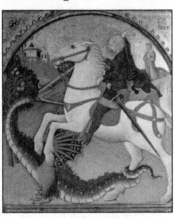

This painting came from the San Cristoforo church which you will have seen earlier on this walk. Sano di Pietro was one of the most popular and successful artists in Siena in the fifteenth century.

Saint George is depicted killing the dragon to save the life of the princess who you can see standing behind.

The dragon is shown wrapping its tail around the leg of the horse which looks ominous, but we know that St George managed to defeat the monster.

His reward was that the King and his people were so impressed that they converted to Christianity.

La Madonna del Latte - Ambrogio Lorenzetti

This is probably the best known painting in the museum.

It's much admired because it shows a very human side of the love between Mary and her baby son, unlike many religious paintings.

The Presentation of the Virgin in the Temple - Sodoma

You will read more about the artist Sodoma later, but for now just enjoy his masterpieces in this museum. They show scenes from the life of the Virgin Mary.

This scene isn't actually in the bible, it's told in a second century gospel. It tells us that Mary's parents had longed for a child for many years. When they got a message from God that one was on the way they were overjoyed. They took Mary, who was just three, to the Temple and dedicated her to God in thanks.

Map 6.5 - When you have finished exploring the museum, cross the square diagonally left to return to the archway on Via Rossi.

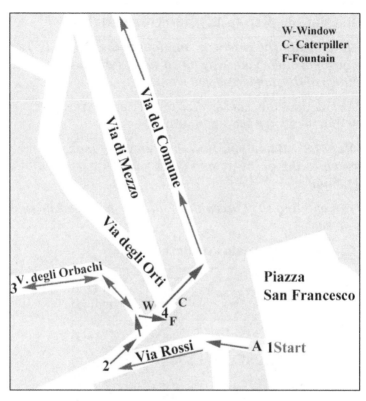

Map 7

Map 7.1 - Go through the archway once more. Walk along Via dei Rossi until you reach a junction where another road joins from the right.

Map 7.2 - Turn right and walk downhill along Via del Comune. After just a few steps you will see an archway into Vicolo degli Orbachi on your left.

Vicolo degli Orbachi was at one time said to be one of the most dangerous places to venture in medieval Siena – but it's perfectly safe now.

Giardino degli Orbachi (Laurel Garden)

Go through the archway and follow the path. To reach the garden, make your way down some stairways to explore as much of the garden as you want.

At one time this garden was full of Laurel trees. It's still a nice spot to rest for a few minutes.

Map 7.3 - When you have had enough, make your way back up to the archway and go through it to return to Via del Comune.

You will find the Caterpillar fountain on the other side of the street.

Caterpillar Fountain and Barbicone

The fountain is decorated with a bust of Barbicone holding a sword. When the Black Death finally left Siena, life was very hard for the survivors, especially for the poorer classes. The people of the Caterpillar Contrada were mostly labourers, and when the government raised yet another tax, it was the last straw.

Barbicone led a rebellion which resulted in the ousting of the government and the establishment of a far fairer system. Life for the poor in Siena improved, and Barbicone is still regarded as a Sienese hero.

Donna alla Finestra

Face away from the fountain and look up to the window in front of you, you will see an intriguing woman looking out of a window. This is Donna all Finestra – Woman at the Window.

If you look closely, you will see that she is looking at a pomegranate suspended in front of her, which has a caterpillar on top of it. There is another caterpillar on the wall to the left of the fountain.

Traditionally the chief adversary of this Contrada is the Contrada of the Giraffe – their neighbours.

Map 7.4 – Stand with the fountain behind you and turn right.

Pass Via Degli Orti on your left and continue straight ahead onto Via del Comune. It will immediately turn sharply left and take you downhill.

Via del Comune is a picturesque old street which is lined with houses leaning against each other.

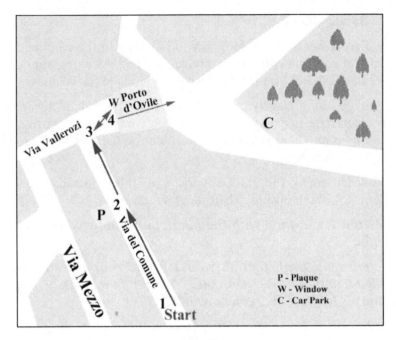

Map 8

Map 8.1 - Stroll down Via del Comune.

As you near the bottom of the hill, spot the memorial plaque on the left-hand side at number 51.

Beppe di Bedo

It commemorates Beppe di Bedo, the rider who won the Palio for the Caterpillar Contrada after 41 years without a win. As you can imagine the Contrada were ecstatic. The plaque translates as:

Here lived Beppe di Bedo,
great contradalid of the twentieth century,
who for the glory of Bruco after 41 years
brought the winning horse

Map 8.2 - Continue to the bottom of the street to a T-junction with Via Vallerozzi.

Via Vallerozzi

You are now in the Wolf Contrada. This residential area used to be inhabited by shepherds and their flocks and it is known as Sheepfold.

You can see one of the ancient city gates, Porto Ovile, on your right.

Map 8.3 - Walk towards the gate.

Porto Ovile

The gate is part of the city battlements and is first mentioned in 1200. It withstood many battles, and was sealed in 1258 and again in 1554 when an attack from Florence was anticipated. It was badly damaged in the 1708 earthquake.

The wooden cross high above you is a replacement made by the craftsmen of the contrade. It replaced the original cross which was too precious to leave to the elements and which is now in the contrada museum.

Look through the little window on the left-hand side of the gate to see another fresco by Sano di Pietro. It's of the Madonna and Child and it's one of the oldest in the city.

Map 8.4 - Go through the archway into the gate chamber, and then step outside the gate.

Have a look at the city walls which are so well preserved. Look to the right to see the San Francesco church which you just visited, sitting high above you.

Near this spot is a very old fountain called the Fonte d'Ovile. Unfortunately Siena has not made it very accessible and it takes a short walk (300 metres) reach it.

If you want to skip it, continue from "Uphill Again" on page 62.

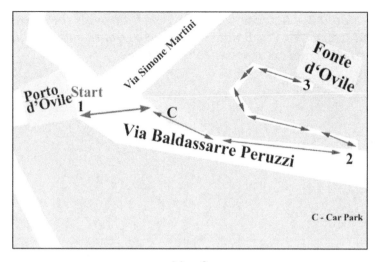

Map 9

Map 9.1 – Otherwise to reach the fountain, stand with the Porto d'Ovile behind you.

You will see a little parking area in front of you, and a sunken tree-filled area behind it. Cross the road in front of you to reach the parking area, and then turn right to walk along Via Baldassarre Peruzzi.

Map 9.2 - After about 100 metres you will reach a side-road on the left which will let you descend into the tree-filled area. Follow the road as it loops back and it will take you to the fountain.

Fonte d'Ovile

The fountain is built of bricks and it has two pointed arches. There is a water trough for animals at the side. There used to be a wash house but has not survived.

It is one of the very oldest of Siena's fountains. It was built in 1262 for use by the many sheep-farms which used to exist near the Porto d'Ovile.

Map 9.3 – Retrace your steps back through the garden and ascend to Via Baldassarre Peruzzi once more. Then turn right and return to the Porto d'Ovile.

Uphill Again

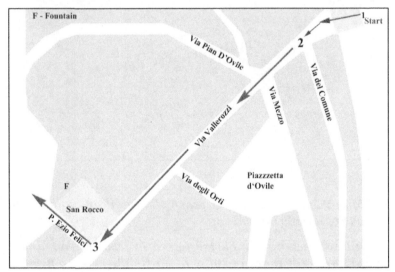

Map 10.1 - Return through the gate and walk straight ahead to start the long climb up Via Vallerozzi, passing Via del Comune on your left

Map 10.2 - Continue to climb, passing Via Mezzo and Via Degli Orti on your left.

Stop when you spot yet another she-wolf on a column on your right. It stands next to the Oratory of San Rocco Confessore

Oratory of San Rocco Confessore

Above the door you can see San Rocco, pointing as he always does, to the sore on his leg. He spent his life nursing victims of the plague but eventually he caught the dreadful disease and died.

Map 10.3 – Turn right at the corner of the Oratory into Piazzetta Enzio Felici.

Walk to the end of the oratory and on your right you will find the striking Wolf fountain.

Wolf Contrada

The Wolf Contrada's prized possession is a photograph of Giuseppe Garibaldi, the leader who did so much to turn the independent Italian city states into one country.

He presented it to the Contrada when they won the Palio in 1867 and it is safely held in the Contrada lodge.

The Wolf Contrada has been less successful this century, as it was Nonna until 2016 when they finally won a palio after 28 years.

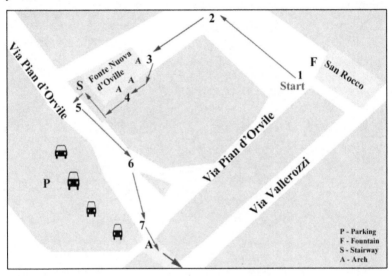

Map 11

Map 11.1 – Stand with the Wolf fountain and the Oratory on your right-hand side. Walk straight ahead and downhill through parked cars to reach a T-junction.

Map 11.2 – Turn left into a square. Head towards the Fonte Nuova O'Ovile which sits straight ahead of you.

Fonte Nuova d'Ovile

The side of the fountain you are looking at has a single grand arch.

Map 11.3 - Go round the left-hand side of the fountain.

Here you will see two more very grand arches. The fountain is built entirely in brick - it looks very like the old Fonte d'Ovile which it replaced, and which you may have just seen.

It was used both by the farmers and the craftsmen who had their workshops here. It was also where the local women would come to wash their linen.

When the Fonte Gaia was built up on the Piazza del Campo, the engineers drew water from the same source which feeds this fountain, so the level of water it provided dropped.

Map 11.4 – Keep walking along the side of the fountain, and then turn right to climb a little flight of steps. You will reach Via Pian d'Orvile.

Beside you stands another stairway which leads up to a house atop the fountain – it was the home of the Fountain Keeper.

Map 11.5 - Stand with both the fountain and the stairway on your left-hand side.

You will see a high brick wall on your right-hand side, and above it is a large car-park. Walk along Via Pian d'Orvile, keeping the wall and car-park on your right.

Map 11.6 - You will reach a fork in the road – go uphill on the right-hand road.

You will see an archway ahead of you. It gives access to a little alleyway called Via del Lavatolo.

Via del Lavatolo – Wash it Street

It provided a handy shortcut which the housewives of Siena used to reach the Fonte Nuova d'Ovile to do their laundry.

Map 11.7 – Go through the archway and follow Via del Lavatolo uphill. You will pop out onto Via Vallerozzi

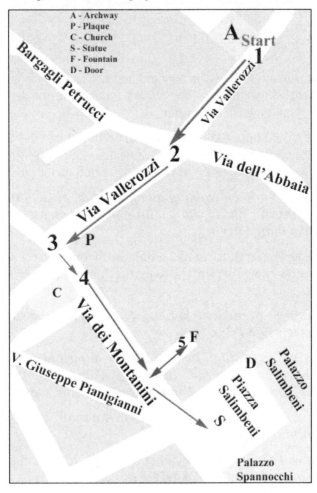

Map 12

Map 12.1 - Turn right onto Via Vallerozzi, still climbing to reach a crossroads.

Map 12.2 - Continue over the crossroads with Via L'Abbadia and Piazzetta Fabio Bargagli Petrucci.

The road will narrow at this point but continue straight ahead towards a staggered crossroads with Via dei Montanini.

Dante Again

On your left hand side, at the corner of Via Vallerozzi and Via dei Montanini, is another plaque commemorating a verse from Dante's Inferno: It has been translated as:

> I was not wise, although I was called Wisdom,
> and I was much more glad of the misfortunes of others
> than of my luck

Dante tells us the story of Sapia Salvani who was born into a Guelph family in Siena (Sapia means wisdom).

She envied the Ghibelline families in Siena who were in power, to the extent that she wanted Siena to be defeated by Florence.

As is usual with Dante's characters, she paid for her envy and disloyalty. She was sent to purgatory, and was placed on the Terrace of Envy where sinners have their eyes sewn shut with wire.

Map 12.3 - Turn left into Via dei Montanini

Via dei Montanini

This road is part of the old Via Francigena, a major route for pilgrims on their way to and from Santiago de Compostela in Spain and Rome. Hospitals, abbeys, and churches were often built along the Via Francigena to help pilgrims along the way.

Via dei Montanini is one of the spots where they would make a break on their journey.

Map 12.4 - Pass the church of Santa Maria delle Nevi on your right.

Just before you walk into Palazzo Spannocchi, take a short detour down the little alley on your left.

Fountain of Abundance

At the far end of the alley stands another of Siena's fountains. It shows a lady surrounded by children. Spot the two cute little frogs at the front.

The fountain was part of an old practical joke inflicted on Siena's adolescent boys. They were told that a lady of the night lived through the door you see next to the fountain, and that she would give any young man his first sexual experience very cheaply. When the victim summoned up his courage and appeared beside the fountain, his tormenters would throw buckets of icy water from the fountain onto him.

At the time of writing the fountain is quite dry, but perhaps when you visit it will be working again.

Map 12.5 – Backtrack to Via dei Montanini and turn left. Walk past the single building on your left to reach pretty Piazza Salimbeni, also on your left.

Palazzo Salimbeni

The central palace on this square is the home of the Salimbeni family. It has beautiful arched windows and what looks like battlements running along the top.

The family was very successful until 1419, when they were found guilty of trying to overthrow the government. Both their palace and their fortune were confiscated by Siena.

Monte dei Paschi di Siena

The Palazzo Salimbeni was sold in 1866 to the Monte dei Paschi bank, and not surprisingly they moved their headquarters into this beautiful building.

It is one of the world's oldest banks and has been trading since the fifteenth century. Its original remit was to help the poor of Siena during bad times, but it evolved into a bank as the years rolled by. Sadly the bank was hit by scandal and money problems in 2013.

You can see the name of the bank above the handsome arched doorway in the far left corner.

Sallustio Bandini

The chap standing in the square is Sallustio Bandini, a very clever seventeenth century priest who you read about earlier in this walk. He championed free trade between cities and the removal of sales taxes and tariffs.

He also collected a huge library of ancient books and manuscripts which he bequeathed to Siena on the condition that the collection was made available to the people. His collection formed the basis of the Siena Library.

Stand face to face with Bandini. On your right stands another lovely palace, the Palazzo Spannocchi.

Palazzo Spannocchi

This palace was built by another successful merchant family who had very useful connections to Pope Pius II. Look right to the top of the palace and you will see a line of heads looking down at you – they are the various Emperors of Rome.

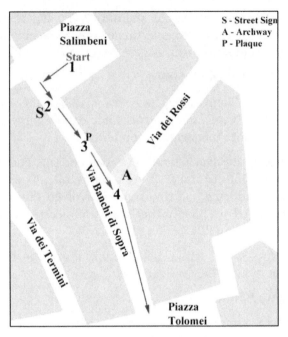

Map 13

Map 13.1 – Stand facing the same direction as Sallustio Bandini.

Walk towards the building in front of you, and then turn left to take a few steps into Banchi di Spora.

Via de Pellicceria

Take a look at the street-sign on you right. You will see that the street actually has two names, Banchi di Sopra and underneath that Via de Pellicceria.

Pellicceria means "furs", and the street got that name in the Middle Ages because this was where the leather and fur workers had their workshops – all gone now of course.

Map 13.2 - Continue along Via Banchi di Sopra and take a look at the arches decorating the wall on your left as you do.

Sienese Arches

For anyone with an interest in architecture, these are classified as "Sienese Arches". A Sienese Arch has a high arc which joins with a lower arc at the bottom to form an equilateral triangle. You can spot more examples as you explore

Continue to reach number 68 on your left. Above it is another plaque.

Federigo Tozzi

It commemorates Federigo Tozzi who is one of Siena's most famous writers. The plaque translates as:

Federigo Tozzi,
one of Italy's greatest novelists,
was born here on 1 January 1883,
in the heart of his city

He grew up in Siena but always felt trapped there, so he left Siena as a teenager to study in Florence and Rome. However Siena never left his heart and he constantly referred to it in his works:

> "Roads that run in all directions, remaining close together, moving apart, they meet up two or three times, they stop; as if they didn't know where to go, with small, lopsided squares, sunken without space, because of all the old buildings upon them"

Tozzi died in 1920 from the Spanish Flu which killed millions. One hundred years later, in 2020, Siena planned a celebration of his life and works. But the world was hit by another terrible pandemic, Covid-19, and the celebrations had to be cancelled. Let's hope Siena doesn't wait another 100 years.

Map 13.3 – A few more steps will bring you to a tall archway on your left. It leads into Via dei Rossi.

Via dei Rossi

It used to be the entrance to another family fortress. It was similar to the Castellare degli Ugurgieri which you saw at the start of the walk. However this one has not survived as well, and has been radically modified over the centuries.

Map 13.4 - Continue along Via Banchi di Sopra and return to Piazza Tolomei which you walked through earlier.

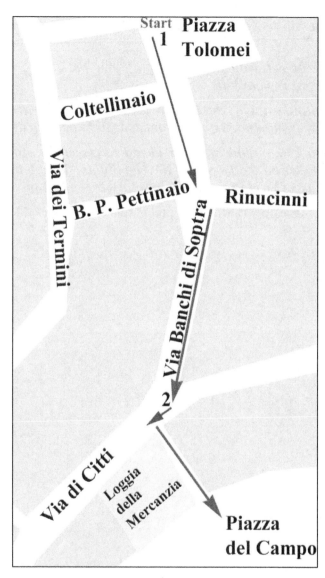

Map 14

Map 14.1 - Once there, walk straight across the square keeping to the right-hand side of the square.

You will leave the square and still be on Via Banchi di Sopra.

The street will swing right as you pass little Vicolo Rinucinni on your left.

Continue along via Banchi di Sopra to return to the three-way junction with Via Banchi di Sotto and Via di Citti.

Map 14.2 - Walk straight ahead to reach the statue of Saint Peter on the Loggia of the Merchants. Turn left down the steps of Vicolo San Pietro to return to the Campo.

You have now reached the end of this walk.

Walk 3 – To the Cathedral and Back

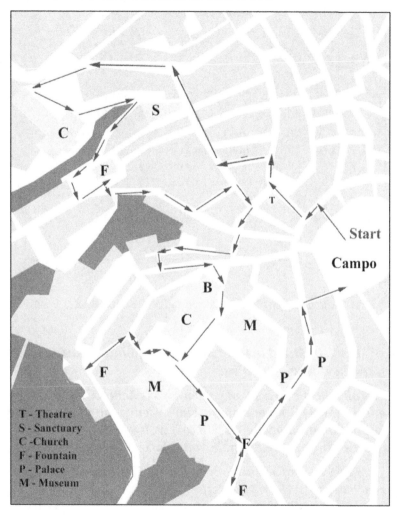

Walk 3 Overview

This walk starts in the Piazza del Campo. It is a circular walk which takes you into the maze of Siena's little streets to reach the Cathedral and back.

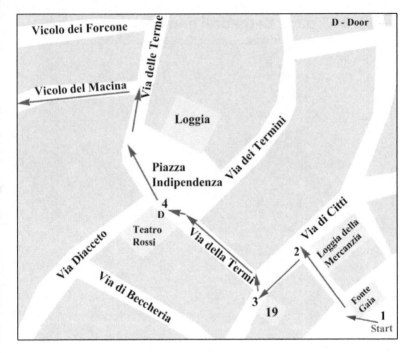

Map 1

Map 1.1 - Stand in front of the Gaia fountain facing away from the Palazza Pubblico.

You will see two small passageways behind the fountain, one on the left and one on the right. Leave the square by the left-hand passageway - it will take you up some steps to Via di Citti which is the main thoroughfare of Siena.

Map 1.2 - Turn left along Via di Citti a short distance to reach number 19 on your left.

Ouch!

Look above the door at number 19. This was where dentist Umberto Gregori practised his trade in the nineteenth century.

He commissioned renowned Sienese sculptor Guido Bainconi, to make this fascinating medallion. It shows two little cherubs, one is the dentist who seems to be wielding a spanner, and the other is the victim. The dentist's name is on the medallion.

Map 1.3 - Backtrack a few steps along Via di Citta to turn left down Via della Terme. It will take you into Piazza Indipendeza.

On your left as you enter the Piazza stands the Teatro dei Rozzi

Teatro dei Rozzi

The original theatre company started in the sixteenth century and was popular enough to attract Pope Leo X and The Holy Roman Emperor to its productions. They didn't have a theatre at that time though, and performed in various places in the city – including the Palazzo Pubblico in the Campo.

The company slowly grew in stature and reputation, so by the early nineteenth century it was planned to build a theatre, and it opened in 1817. It was damaged in WWII and it closed its doors after a final show in 1945 for the allied troops. Happily it reopened in 1998.

Look above the door and you can see the coat of arms of the Rozzi Company. The word Rozzi translates as Rough.

Below that you can see an old cork tree with a young sapling growing from the tree's root.   It represents the company's vision – to stage "rough" pieces of work, i.e. those from non-standard and perhaps unconventional sources.

Across the tree runs the company's motto which roughly translates as:

Those who stay here gain what they lose

It is trying to say, that those who join the Rough Company improve and lose their own roughness.

Car Power

Opposite the theatre is a rather grand Loggia with a sad story.

The Loggia was part of a War Memorial for Italian Independence which was constructed in the late nineteenth century. Originally a commemorative statue stood in front of it, however the statue was doomed.

Firstly it caused indignation as it depicted a woman standing over a dying lion. The lion represented the lost soldiers of Siena but to the general public it was defeatist and was therefore hated.

But more importantly the statue gobbled up coveted parking space. Yes, the Italian love of their cars resulted in the statue being uprooted and placed in a park further out of town. So now all that is left is a rather orphaned loggia. Perhaps one day the cars will be banished and the statue returned.

Map 1.4 – Face the Loggia. Leave the square by Via delle Terme which continues along the left-hand side of the loggia.

Take the first left into Vicolo del Macin. Walk downhill to reach a T-junction with Via Galluzza.

Map 3

Via Galluzza

Look left to admire the eight arches which criss-cross this medieval street – you will walk under them later.

Map 2.1 - For now turn right. Walk downhill passing Vicolo del Forcone on your right. You will reach a crossroads with Via Santa Caterina.

Map 2.2 - Cross Via Santa Caterina and start to climb up Costa Sant'Antonio. You will soon reach the iron gateway to the Santa Caterina Sanctuary on your left. It's usually very busy.

Santa Caterina

Caterina was a local girl who worshipped at the church of San Domenico, perhaps to escape her twenty-four brothers and sisters!

She started having visions as a child and they more or less continued for the rest of her life. As she became older and more devoted to God she started to fast; she is mentioned as an example in the book Holy Anorexia by Rudolph Bell. She also endured scourging, inflicting terrible punishment on herself to mimic the suffering of Jesus before his crucifixion.

She claimed to have had many visions including a mystical marriage with Jesus. A mystical marriage, according to the church, is a vision where Jesus tells the visionary that he takes her for his bride. She also received the stigmata while praying at a church in Pisa.

Caterina became almost a hermit living in her family home in a single small room. She finally re-joined the world, and became very outspoken in church affairs and a great writer. Her religious texts are seen as one of the highlights of the medieval world. She was also a great favourite of the Pope, she even managed to persuade him to quit civilised French Avignon and return the papacy to the bedlam of Rome.

She spent her last few years in Rome where she finally starved to death at only 33. She is much loved by religious Italian women. She became the patron saint of Italy and was also the first female "Doctor of the Church"- a very senior type of Saint.

Santa Caterina Sanctuary

Go through the gate into the courtyard. The beautiful arched porch running along the building was added in 1939 when Caterina became the patron saint of Italy. Each municipality in Italy donated money to buy a single brick, and the porch was constructed between 1941 and 1947 – the war held things up.

If you decide to venture in you will see the following:

Chiesa del Crocifisso – The church of the Crucifx

This church was built over Caterina's garden. Inside you will see the crucifix which Caterina was gazing at in Pisa when she was given the stigmata – five wounds just like Christ.

Interestingly Caterina prayed that only she should see the stigmata, so they became invisible until she died when they reappeared. In fact the church only officially recognised the stigmata in 1623 two centuries after she died.

Oratorio della Cucina – Oratory of the Kitchen

This was the family kitchen and is now decorated with frescoes, all telling of Caterina's eventful life and good works.

It was also the scene of another of Caterina's miracles. Look below the altar and you will see a grate which hides a hearth. Caterina was having a vision when she fell onto the burning hearth but was not hurt.

Oratorio della Camera – Caterina's cell

Also in the house you can see Caterina's cell, where she lived for three years, more or less as a hermit, starving herself and enduring terrible scourging. She rarely left the cell during this time and then only to visit the Chapel of the Vaults in the San Dominica church.

Map 2.3 - With the gateway to the Sanctuary behind you, turn left to climb up Costa Sant'Antonio to reach a T-junction with Via della Sapienza.

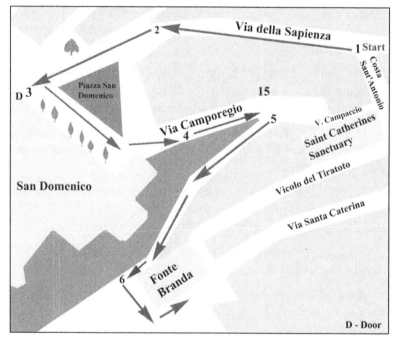

Map 3

La Casa della Sapienza

Sapienza means wisdom and the road takes its name from the La Casa della Sapienza, the House of Wisdom, which is now Siena's public library.

It was built in 1759 to house the collection of Sallustio Bandini, the scholarly priest whose statue you saw on walk two in Piazza Salimbeni. If you were to turn right along Via della Sapienza you would reach the library.

Map 3.1 – Instead turn left along Via della Sapienza. Eventually you will emerge onto a large square dominated by the Basilica di San Domenico.

Basilica di San Domenico

This church was started in the thirteenth century and was almost complete when Santa Caterina was born in the same neighbourhood. Its distinctive red brick tower can be spotted from all over town.

The Dominicans who built it followed the teachings of Saint Dominic, and were known as the Black Friars because of their black cloaks. They encouraged contemplation and learning.

Map 3.2 - Walk towards the basilica. At the time of writing the tourist entrance is directly ahead of you at the end of the basilica.

As you approach the basilica have a look at the church tower. It was built in 1125 and was originally taller but lost some height in the earthquake in the eighteenth century.

The church has also survived two devastating fires and occupation by the Spanish Army in the sixteenth century.

It has now been restored back to the original Dominican plan.

Go into the Basilica

You might be a little let down when you enter as it is rather sparse in decoration, but persevere as there are things worth seeing. The church is most famous for the story and the remains of Santa Caterina.

When Caterina became a saint in 1461, all her most important writings and belongings were placed behind a painting in the sacristy. Since then, they have been stashed in a museum – I think it would have been much more intriguing to have left them in the church.

The Chapel of Vaults

The chapel to the Vaults is on the right as you enter, and is where the nuns and holy women prayed. It was here that Caterina had so many of her mystical experiences.

She would lean on the octagonal pillar on the open side of the chapel and her followers would faithfully record her continuing conversations with Jesus Christ. These conversations formed the Dialogue on Divine Providence, her most important work.

The chapel also holds the only portrait of Santa Caterina. If you are facing the chapel it is on the left hand wall; she is holding a lily. Take a good look at it before you reach the Cappella di Santa Caterina a little further on.

With the Chapel of Vaults behind you walk straight ahead to find the Capella di Santa Caterina on your right.

Cappella di Santa Caterina

Move on to the Cappella di Santa Caterina where the walls are frescoed with events from the saint's life. They are mostly by Sodoma.

He was a colourful character who spent most of his working life in Siena. His real name was Giovanni Antonio Bazzi, and at one point was married and fathered two children. However he led an unconventional life and "Sodoma" was probably an insult from other artists who disapproved. Bazzi thought it was wonderful and adopted it as his working name.

The star of the show is Santa Caterina's head which you can see in a gilt case on the very ornate marble altar. Her finger is also on display - the rest of her is in Rome. Some people find the head quite shocking.

Caterina's head has had a few mishaps. It was almost lost in a fire in 1531. Later while in a religious procession, the locals tried to pinch it and dropped it. However it has survived as you can see.

Fainting and Ecstasy of Santa Caterina - Sodoma

Sodoma painted the fresco "Fainting and Ecstasy of Santa Caterina" which surrounds the chapel altar. It has been said that Caterina is so lifelike in it that she seems to be breathing!

Work on the Cappella di Santa Caterina was continued by Vanni. Find his painting of "Santa Caterina exorcising a Possessed Woman" which is very dramatic!

Santa Barbara - Matteo di giovanni

You should also try to find the glowing "St Barbara Enthroned with Angels and Saints Mary Magdalene and Catherine". It is in the first chapel to the right of the altar.

It shows two angels laying a crown on Saint Barbara's head. The Catherine portrayed is Saint Catherine of Alexandria – not the local Catherine!!

So who was Saint Barbara? She was the daughter of a pagan nobleman, who had her horrifically tortured because she would not denounce God and return to worshipping the trees. Finally she was executed by her father – who was immediately struck down by lightning and fried.

When you have seen enough, make your way back outside.

Map 3.3 - With the Basilica door behind you, turn right. Keep the line of tall poplar trees on your right-hand side and walk downhill on Piazza San Domenico.

You will pass another of the Basilica's doors on your right.

When you reach the hedge, turn left along Via del Camporegio and walk downhill a little further.

Enjoy the great view over the red rooftops of Siena, with the Mangia Tower on the Campo to the left, and the Cathedral to the right.

Map 3.4 – Continue down Via del Camporegio as far as number 15 on your left – it's about halfway along.

Map 3.5 - You will see a fork in the road. Take the stepped right-hand route. It will take you all the way down the hill, with the Basilica towering overhead on your right.

Map 3.6 - At the bottom of the steps, turn left to reach the Fonte Branda.

Fonte Branda

Most tourists of Siena are unaware that underneath the city is a 25 kilometre network of tunnels which has brought running water into Siena's homes and fountains since the 12th century.

This system of tunnels is called the "Bottini". Both this fountain and the Fonte Gaia in the Campo are connected to the Bottini.

The Fonte Branda is a water catchment construction built underneath San Domenica. It has three cisterns, the first was for drinking water, the second was for watering animals, and the third was for washing.

You are in the Contrada of the Goose right now and they decided they may as well use the Fonte Branda as their territorial fountain, as they would be hard pushed to build a better one.

Dante and the Fonte Branda

The Fonte Branda is one of the most interesting of Siena's many fountains; it even gets a mention by Dante in his Inferno:

> **But if I here could see the tristful soul Of Guido,**
> **or Alessandro, or their brother,**
> **For Branda's Fount I would not give the sight.**

These words are said by a counterfeiter who has been sent down to Hell. He is so lonely that if he could have just one of his friends down there with him, he would sacrifice all the fresh water from Siena's Branda fountain.

Face the fountain and take a few steps back. Look left to see the city wall and the Porta di Fontebranda some distance away.

Porta di Fontebranda

You are looking at the lowest point of the city wall. It stands 32 meters below the Campo and 73 meters below the highest point of the wall at San Quirico.

If you were to walk through the gate you would see the IHS symbol of the fire and brimstone priest Bernadine who you may have already read about on walk 2.

There used to be a much larger fortified gate beyond the Porta di Fontebranda, similar to the gate you may have already seen on Walk 2, but it has not survived.

A Choice

This walk now takes you back up to the Cathedral which you can see high above you.

You have a choice on how to tackle the hill to get up there – escalator or walk.

Escalator

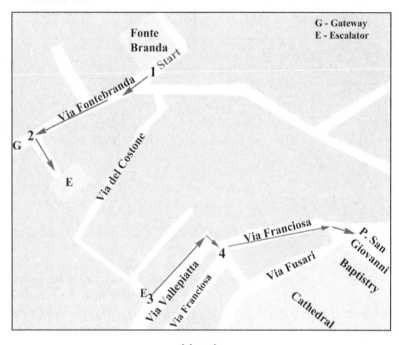

Map 4

Siena has recently installed a series of escalators which will take you uphill and deposit you quite near the Cathedral.

Map 4.1 - To use the escalator, face the fountain and turn left to walk towards the Porta di Fontebranda.

Map 4.2 - You will find the path and signpost to the escalator on your left just before you reach the gate. Take the escalators up.

Map 4.3 – The escalators will deposit you onto Via di Vallepiatta. Turn left to walk along Via di Vallepiatta. It will turn sharply right to reach a crossroads.

Map 4.4 - Turn left into Via Franciosa which will curve right and take you onto Piazza San Giovanni.

Re-join the walk at "Piazza San Giovanni" on Page 94.

Walk

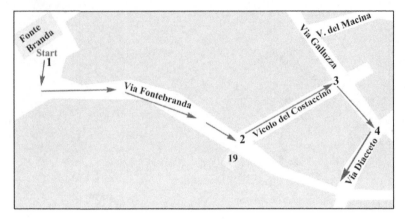

Map 5

Map 5.1 - If on the other hand you want to see a bit more of medieval Siena and you don't mind the climb, face away from the Fonte Branda fountain, turn left, and go uphill on Via Fontebranda.

Your route will now take you through a series of tiny streets. You have entered the Contrada of the Forest – whose symbol is a tree under which a rhinoceros stands.

Map 5.2 - Take the first left into little Vicolo del Costaccino. You will find it on your left-hand side opposite number 19.

Map 5.3 - After a bit more climbing you will reach a T-junction with Via della Galluzza which you strolled down earlier.

Turn right into Via della Galluza.

Via della Galluza

The name of the street comes from the domestic bird market which used to be here – gallo means rooster in Italian.

You now get to pass under those arches you saw earlier in the walk.

You will reach a crossroads with Via Diacetta.

Map 5.4 – Turn right into Via Diacceto.

Via Diacceta

This little street was used as an early freezer because it was so shaded.

It may seem improbable if you visit Siena on a hot day, but the locals packed ice into pits in winter in this street for a nice cool drink in the summer and to safely store meat.

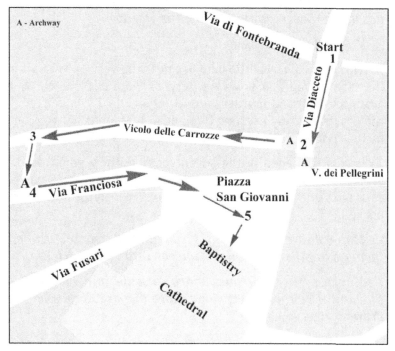

Map 6

Map 6.1 - Cross over Via di FonteBranda which you see below you and which you climbed up just a few minutes ago.

You will get a good view of the San Domenico Basilica as you do.

Continue along Via Diacceto. You will see an archway straight ahead of you, DON'T go through it.

Map 6.2 - Instead turn right through an old gated archway on your right-hand side. This is little Vicolo delle Carrozze, the alley of the Carriages.

Keep waking straight ahead along Vicolo delle Carrozze, passing under a couple of arches as you do.

Vicolo delle Carrozze

This atmospheric little lane lies near the very oldest part of the city. Long ago it was a very dangerous place to walk around – theft and murder were common. In 1298 Siena took the drastic action of sealing the lane at both ends to avoid any further crimes being committed there.

It was reopened in the seventeenth century when the La Scala hotel opened its doors nearby. The alley was where carriage's for the lords and ladies who stayed at the hotel were parked.

Map 6.3 - Near the end of Vicolo delle Carrozze, turn left through another archway to emerge into Via Franciosca.

Map 6.4 Turn left once more to walk into Piazza San Giovanni. You will pass some more Sienese arches on Via Franciosa as you do.

Piazza San Giovanni

You are now in the Contrada of the Eagle. Their symbol is a double-headed black eagle holding an orb, a sword and a sceptre. Traditionally, its residents were notaries.

It is another Noble contrada. It got that honour from Charles V of the Hapsburg Empire who enjoyed his visit to the Eagle Contrada in the sixteenth century.

The Contrada museum is home to the oldest surviving Palio banner, dating from 1719.

The Baptistery

Dominating the Piazza San Giovanni is the baptistery which was built in the fourteenth century.

A baptistery is rather obviously where baptisms take place and are sometimes individual stand-alone buildings by themselves e.g. in Florence. However Siena's baptistery is attached to the rear of the cathedral.

If you don't want to visit the baptistery, jump to "Leaving the Baptistery" on page *98.*

Map 6.5 - Climb the steps to enter the Baptistery.

If you haven't pre-booked your tickets you may have to join a long queue to get them.

Inside the Baptistery

The inside of the Baptistery is beautifully decorated with a riot of frescoes.

The Font

One of the main attractions is the wonderful hexagonal baptismal font made of bronze, marble and enamel.

It is decorated with panels representing the life of John the Baptist and they were made by the greatest sculptors of the day including Quercia and Ghiberti who were very famous. The scenes depicted are:

Annunciation to Zacharias
Birth of John the Baptist
Baptist Preaching
Baptism of Christ
Arrest of John the Baptist
The Feast of Herod

The Feast of Herod by Donatello

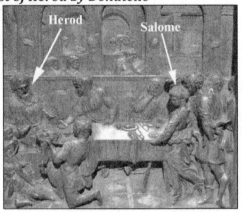

Find the panel depicting a shocked King Herod being presented with the head of John the Baptist. His shock is surprising since he agreed to give the head to Salome if she danced for him. Salome stands to the right of the scene, watching the drama.

Why did Salome ask for his head? Her mother, Herodias, was married to King Herod but the marriage was not legal in Jewish law, because Herodias had previously been married to Herod's brother and had divorced him.

John the Baptist shamed them by declaring them adulterers, so Herod tossed John into prison and Herodias planned her revenge. She persuaded her beautiful daughter Salome to dance for Herod if he would have The Baptist killed.

This panel is one of the first examples of an artist using perspective to let the viewer see depth in an image. You can see clearly that the arches and people get smaller the further "back" in the image they are.

Between the panels stand statues of the virtues. Faith and Hope are also by Donatello.

Hope is shown raising her hands towards God.

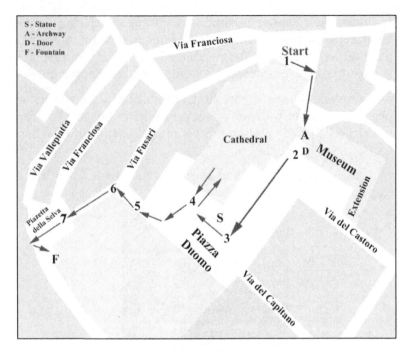

Map 7

When you have seen enough, leave the Baptistery.

Leaving the Baptistery

Map 7.1 – With the Baptistery door behind you, turn right and then right again to go up the steps on the side of the baptistery.

When you reach the top, go through the archway in front of you.

A Failed Expansion

What you see on your left and behind you are the remnants of the planned cathedral expansion.

Take a look at the size of the existing cathedral on you right-hand side. The plan was to turn the existing cathedral into the transept of the new cathedral! It would have been truly enormous. This was all part of the never-ending competition with Florence. Siena planned the biggest cathedral in the world.

However the Black Death arrived and 80% of the population perished so not surprisingly expansion stopped.

You can actually climb up a spiral staircase to the top of the extension and get a great view of Siena. It's accessed via the Cathedral Museum, so perhaps that's another reason you should visit the museum.

You can see the Cathedral Museum door on your left.

If you are not interested in visiting the museum or climbing the extension, continue from "Leaving the Museum" on page 104. Otherwise, head for the museum entrance.

Cathedral Museum

The museum is home to the most treasured piece of art in Siena, Duccio's Maestà. At the time of writing it's on the first floor, but check when you go in.

Duccio's Maestà

Duccio was a very famous artist born in Siena. One of his works, The Stoclet Madonna, was purchased by the New York Met for an astonishing 45 million dollars in 2004, at the time the most expensive purchase ever by a museum.

A Maesta is a sort of medieval collage, a collection of paintings which tell a story. This one was originally the Cathedral altarpiece and legend tells us when Duccio finished the work back in 1311, it was carried in procession to the altar by the clergy, government officials, and every last citizen in Siena.

It is considered one of the most important late medieval paintings in all of Europe. It managed to survive intact until 1711 when it was split up and placed on two altars. It never recovered as some panels were damaged and some just disappeared. There are still several panels in foreign museums so it's unlikely ever to be reassembled. The misplaced panels are:

- Angel - Philadelphia Museum of Art
- Archangel Gabriel - Huis Bergh, The Netherlands
- Angel - Mount Holyoke Museum, Massachusetts
- The Coronation of the Virgin - Szépmûvészeti Múzeum, Budapest
- The Annunciation - National Gallery, London
- The Nativity with the Prophets Isaiah and Ezekiel- National Gallery of Art, Washington DC
- Temptation of Christ on the Mountain – Frick collection, New York
- Calling of SS. Peter and Andrew - National Gallery of Art, Washington DC
- Christ and the Samaritan Woman - Museo Nacional Thyssen-Bornemisza, Madrid
- Healing of the Blind Man – National Gallery, London
- The Transfiguration - National Gallery, London
- The Raising of Lazarus – Kimbell Art Museum, Texas

The Marriage Feast at Cana - Duccio di Buoninsegna

This panel shows Jesus on the left with Mary beside him. On his other side are five apostles as the other seven hadn't been recruited at that point. Jesus has just turned the water in the jars into wine.

Sala della Madonna degli Occhi Grossi

Next, find the much older "Madonna with the big eyes" – a great name for a painting!

It was painted in the thirteenth century and it looks very different to the religious paintings we are used to in Europe – especially the figure of Jesus.

The Madonna was ousted from the Cathedral altarpiece and replaced by Duccio's Maesta. She forgave Siena that indignity and answered the people's prayers when the army of Florence appeared on the horizon. Ungratefully the Sienese moved her once again, out of the cathedral altogether and into the museum, which I think is rather a sad ending.

Saint Bernardino preaching in the Campo - Sano di Pietro

You may have already read about the fire and brimstone Saint Bernardino. This painting shows him in the campo preaching to an entranced audience. Behind him is the Palazzo Pubblico.

There are many more interesting pieces of religious art to browse around. Don't miss going upstairs for a fantastic view of the city from the extension.

When you've have seen enough, exit.

Leaving the Museum

Map 7.2 - With the museum door behind you, turn left to walk along the side of the Cathedral.

As you do, take a look behind you to get a good view of the tower.

The Cathedral Tower

The number of windows in the tower increments on each floor and the tower is topped by a pyramid. The tower has six bells and the oldest was cast in the twelfth century.

Map 7.3 – When you reach the cathedral steps, turn right to stand at the bottom of the steps facing the Cathedral.

The Cathedral

The cathedral sits on the highest point of old Siena, and was built on top of a pagan temple dedicated to Minerva. Its construction carried on throughout the 13th century. It's a pyjama affair in white and greenish black stripes – a style popular all over Tuscany. There is a dash of pink around the doors, perhaps just to add a bit of contrast.

A link to Rome

Find the column topped with the she-wolf breast-feeding Romulus and Remus at the top of the steps.

The black and white stripes which adorn the cathedral are very fitting as black and white are also the colours of Siena's coat of arms. The colours of the city refer again to the legendary city founders, Senius and Aschius. Apparently Aschius rode a black horse and Senius rode a white one. You will see the black and white coat of arms on many buildings as you stroll around.

The Cathedral Facade

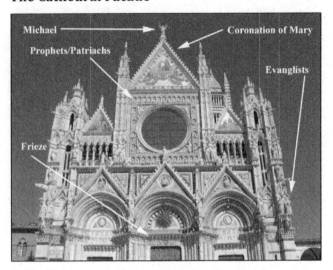

Before you enter the cathedral, stand back and gaze at the façade which is full of intricate detail.

Pisano was a famous architect and sculptor. He didn't actually come from Siena but spent most of his working life there. He is most famous for his work on Siena cathedral and he even has an asteroid name after him "7313 Pisano". He was responsible for much of the statuary you see.

Right at the top of the cathedral the Archangel Michael stands with his spear.

Beneath Michael is the colourful Coronation of Mary. This is the moment Jesus places a crown on his mother's head making her the Queen of Heaven, with a host of angels watching from below the cloud.

Below that is a large round window surrounded by 36 patriarchs and prophets-

Now drop your gaze down a bit to the right of the triangular pediments over the doors. There you can see The Evangelists (they wrote the first four books of the New Testament) gazing down at you.

Finally below that and over the central door is a frieze showing the life of the Virgin Mary.

Sator Square

If you have the time and are interested you can try to find a Sator Square which is on the north side of the cathedral.

Face the front of the cathedral and go down its left-hand side. The sator square is visible from ground level and is just above head height, but it's quite small so you need to look carefully.

A Sator square contains five words arranged in such a way as to be readable in four directions. No one is sure what they actually mean. They appear all over Europe in old buildings, from Sweden to Portugal to Italy – there's even one in Cirencester, England.

Once you've spotted it, make your way back to the front of the cathedral.

If you don't want to go inside the cathedral, continue this walk from "Leaving the Cathedral" on page 117.

Cathedral Interior

Otherwise step inside and catch your jaw as it drops - they don't come much better than this.

The black and white pyjama style continues inside to eye-popping effect. The church is topped by a vaulted roof decorated in blue with golden stars, itself topped by Bernini's gilded lantern, which shines downwards like the sun.

As you explore and look around you will see many popes, emperors, and prophets gazing down at you from on high.

The Marble Pavement

The marble mosaic floor is one of the most ornate in Italy. Vasari, who was a renowned artist and architect from Florence, is quoted as saying that the floor was the:

most beautiful, largest
and most magnificent floor ever made

The marbles evoke stories from the bible and from mythology. Sadly the entire floor can only be seen for six to ten weeks around September and for the rest of the year it's covered and only a few panels are on a roped- off display – so plan your visit well!

The first mosaic you see as you enter the Cathedral is of a mystical figure, Ermete Trismegisto, who is thought to have lived around the same time as Moses. He represents wisdom and knowledge and wrote many papers and books.

If you ever visit Amsterdam's Bibliotheca Philosophica Hermetica you can see a treasure-trove of ancient books and manuscripts including the Corpus Hermeticum. It is a book from the fifteenth century - a compilation of some of those ancient scripts by Ermete Trismegisto.

The She-wolf and other animals

The mosaic of the She Wolf and Romulus and Remus is one of the first floor mosaics you will see as you enter. Encircling the she-wolf are emblems of other famous Tuscan cities, Pisa, Lucca etc.   It is the second oldest mosaic from 1373.

Allegory of the Hill of Wisdom

A little further on lies Fortune. It depicts Fortune as a young woman delicately balancing on a globe and a ship, perhaps telling us how unpredictable life is.

However Fortune has landed a group of men on an island and their task is to climb to the top to find Wisdom – who is seated in a garden. The chap on the right who is tossing his fortune into the sea is Crates. He lived in Crete and came from a very wealthy family, but gave all his riches away and chose to live amongst the poor. The chap on the left is Socrates, the Greek philosopher.

So the moral is that life is difficult and full of perils, but at the end is wisdom and peace.

Massacre of the Innocents

One panel which should not to be missed, if it is on view, is Matteo di Giovanni's Massacre of the Innocents. From the Main door, it lies about halfway along the church on the left hand side. It illustrates the murder of all Jewish baby boys by order of King Herod - he was making sure that the prophesised messiah was removed before he became a problem.

The artist was obsessed by this incident and he produced several works on the same theme in other churches. You will see another version if you visit Santa Maria della Scala a little later. This version is strange in that the smiling victims all seem to be positively happy about the event.

The pulpit

You can't miss the eye-catching pulpit which is the oldest work in the cathedral. It sits on granite, porphyry, and green marble columns, themselves supported by marble lions. It's made of glowing Carrera marble and was carved by Pisano and his son; it is considered Pisano's masterpiece.

The pulpit panels show us the Life of Christ. It is done in what's called a chiaroscuro effect, which uses light and dark to give it depth and liveliness. Look carefully and you will see a different expression on each character's face – wonderful.

The Chigi Chapel

From the main door, the Chapel of the Madonna del Voto, informally called the Chigi Chapel, is on the right hand side of the Cathedral about halfway down.

The Chigi family were one of Siena's most powerful families – Fabio Chigi became Pope Alexander VII. With power comes wealth and influence - the Chigi palace in Rome is where the Italian Government sits.

The chapel glows with blue lapis lazuli and is topped with a gilded dome. It was designed by Bernini the greatest architect/sculptor of the day. It is the final and most luxurious addition to the cathedral.

The Madonna you see is much revered by the Contrada. In times past the Sienese prayed to the Madonna when danger approached, usually in the form of the Florentine army. They believe she has personally interceded more than once so they pay homage to her every year, perhaps unaware that the original Madonna is in the museum - or perhaps it doesn't matter.

Mary Magdalene - Bernini

Find the beautiful Bernini statue of Mary Magdalene. There is gentleness to it which you don't often see in biblical statuary. It shows Mary near the end of her life when she lived as a hermit and tried to atone for her sins. Her foot is resting on a bowl which represents the bowl of ointment she used to wash Christ's feet.

Chapel of San Giovanni Battista

The chapel of John the Baptist is on the other side of the Cathedral, almost directly opposite the Chigi Chapel.

Centre-stage you will find a bronze statue of John the Baptist, looking wild in his wilderness skins, by Donatello.

In the fifteenth century, Pope Pius II decided to give the right arm of John the Baptist to the cathedral, and this chapel was built to house such an important relic. It is still here but it is hidden most of the year, and it only appears for public viewing a few days before the saint's day on June 24th.

It's housed in a silver reliquary and three keys are needed to unlock it; one is held by the Municipality of Siena, one by the Cathedral, and one by the Cathedral Museum.

The Piccolomini library

The Piccolomini library is also on the left hand side of the Cathedral. It was added to celebrate the life and book collection of Pope Pious II. It was commissioned by his nephew Pope Pious III – it obviously runs in the family.

As you enter, get ready for a change of mood, as the black and white of the Cathedral gives way to a rainbow of colour. The walls portray the life of the Pope on beautiful frescoes.

Ambassador at the Scottish Court

The scenes are:

- Leaving for the Council of Basel with a storm raging in the background

- Ambassador at the Scottish Court with Scotland depicted as a Mediterranean hotspot

- Crowned court poet by Emperor Frederick III

- Meets Pope Eugene IV

- As bishop of Siena, presents Emperor Frederick III with his bride-to-be Eleanora of Portugal.

- Becomes a cardinal in 1456

- Becomes pontiff in 1458

- Pius II proclaims a new crusade in 1459

- Pius II canonizes Santa Caterina of Siena in 1461

- Pius II visits Ancona to launch the new crusade

Finally, in the middle of the library you will find the famous statue of the Three Graces. It's a Roman copy of a Greek original and worth a look and a snap. It's been copied many times by many artists. I always think they look a bit tiddly, perhaps coming home from a girl's night out.

The Piccolomini altar

Near the entrance to the Piccolomini Library you will see the very solemn Piccolomini altar which was intended to be part of the tomb of pope Pious III – the chap who commissioned the library. However he only lasted twenty-six days before dying of a leg ulcer.

The altar has many statues but four of them are worth looking at as they were sculpted by a young Michelangelo; look to the left to see St Gregory and St Paul, and to the right stands St Peter and St Pius.

The Main Altar

The kaleidoscopic Cathedral altar contains four beautiful bronze angels, each holding a candle aloft.

The Crypt

If you have time, make your way down to the crypt. It's a bit of a misnomer as it was never actually used for burials. It was decorated as lavishly as the cathedral but then for some reason it was used as a storeroom, filled with rubbish, and closed.

It has been opened and restored and you can now enjoy it in a way the Sienese haven't for about 600 years.

Leaving the Cathedral

Once back outside, stand in front of the Cathedral with your back to the Cathedral door.

If you would like to see another of the Contrada fountains, it's only a short detour. If not, continue from "Santa Maria della Scala" on Page 118.

Fountain detour

Map 7.4 - To see the Contrada fountain, face away from the cathedral door, descend the steps, and cross the square diagonally right.

Map 7.5 - Leave the square by turning right into Via dei Fusari.

Map 7.6 - You will find an archway and a flight of steps in the corner on the left. It will take you down along a rather dark corridor called Vicolo di San Girolamo to Piazzetta della Selva.

Map 7.7 - When you reach the bottom of the steps, walk straight ahead towards the wall ahead of you. Once there turn round to find the fountain in the corner behind you.

Contrada of the Forest

You are now back in the Contrada of the Forest. The fountain displays the contrada symbol, a rhinoceros standing under a tree. A rhinoceros does seem an odd choice for an Italian institution, but apparently it represents Strength and the Wilderness.

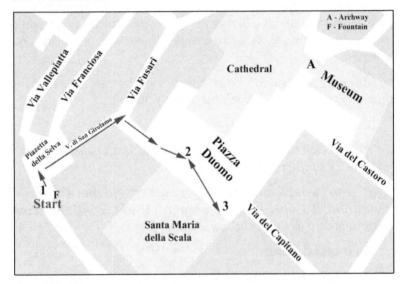

Map 8.1 – Back-track up the stairs on Vicolo di San Girolamo. At the top, turn right to return to the Cathedral steps.

Map 8.2 - Stand at the bottom of the steps with the main door of the cathedral behind you. Look diagonally to your left to see Santa Maria della Scala.

Santa Maria della Scala

This building was one of the oldest hospitals surviving in the world and was only decommissioned in the 1980s. It is now a museum.

Legend tells us that it started as an orphanage and later became a place where pilgrims on the nearby Via Francigena to Rome could stop and be cared for. It was then extended to become a hospital caring for the poor and the sick, and as you can imagine it was used extensively during the dreadful plague.

It grew in stature and importance, and Siena's artists decorated it accordingly. It's actually the third most important building for art in Siena, after the Cathedral and the Palazzo Pubblico.

Behind that door is a wonderland of exhibits and the astonishing building itself is worth a visit with many floors full of ancient chapels, crypts and arcades.

> Note, it is a very large building and you might find yourself spending some time there. If you have time, you might want to return another day just to explore it.

If you don't wish to visit the museum right now, continue this walk from "Leaving Santa Maria della Scala" on Page 123.

Otherwise venture in and explore.

Pilgrim's hall

Enjoy the beautiful arched Pilgrim's Hall which is covered in frescos depicting the hospital's history. You can see the doctors examining the sick for various ailments, and the fearful expression on the faces of the patients – after all medieval medicine was frequently a dreadful affair.

Storia *del Beato Sorore* - Vecchietta

One of the first frescoes you see in the Pilgrims Hall is called the Storia del Beato Sorore.

Storia del Beato Sorore

Sorore is said to have founded the orphanage which eventually became the Santa Maria della Scala.

The fresco illustrates the dream which Sorore's mother is said to have had before her daughter was born. She dreamt that her daughter would found an orphanage, not only to save abandoned children, but to teach them of God and raise them as good Christians.

You can see the saved children climbing a ladder to heaven to be welcomed by Mary. Sorore stands on the right, being given an orphan to take care of.

Some believe that the hospital complex may have derived its name from this painting - scala means ladder. Less romantic thinkers believe it is just derived from its position - opposite the cathedral steps.

It should be said that many historians classify the story of Sorore as urban myth, a story invented to explain the origin of the orphanage/hospital complex.

Massacre of the Innocents - Matteo di Giovanni

Here you can see the little murdered children lying on the steps, and the vicious expression of Herod as he watches their death. The desperate expressions of the mothers as their children are killed are heart-breaking.

Church of Santissima Annunziata

Don't miss the 13th century Church of Santissima Annunziata as it is really worth seeing.

Your eyes will be drawn to the wonderfully colourful frescoed apse, which shows us the story of the Pool of Bethesda.

Pool of Bethesda

The pool is mentioned in the bible as a magical healing place in Jerusalem. However when Jesus visited the pool, he came across an old man who was still unable to walk despite having sat in the waters. Jesus told the man to "Pick up your bed and Walk" – which he did!

Make sure you don't miss the beautiful bronze Risen Christ which stands in front of it.

An excavation in 1999 found a crypt below this church which contained three perfectly mummified bodies.

Hayloft

This is a small room where you'll find the original marble Fonte Gaia and its nude statues - the one in the Campo is of course a copy.

Oratory of Santa Caterina of the Night

Also on this floor is the Oratory of Santa Caterina of the Night, a beautiful chapel where Santa Caterina prayed when she was not nursing the sick and dying.

The Treasure

The treasure of Santa Maria della Scala is now in the Warehouses of the Corticella, which you can also visit on this level. The Corticella were the lands owned by the hospital all around Siena.

The treasure is a set of relics in gold and silver containers gathered together by the various Byzantine emperors in Constantinople as they hunted for a piece of the True Cross. A merchant from Florence bought them in the fourteenth century for 3,000 Florins - a vast amount of money in those days. The relics were put on show for the people every year.

Il Sacro Chiodo della Croce

The highlight is the silver 'Il Sacro Chiodo della Croce' which Emperor Constantine himself owned. It is supposed to be an intact nail which was used to nail Christ to the Cross.

Once it was placed in Siena, other beautiful items were donated by rich Sienese families. There is a massive Gospel of parchment paper beautifully decorated and bound in a silver cover.

The Basement

Finally down in the basement is the Archaeological Museum worth visiting for its location in a labyrinth of tunnels which were originally storerooms.

Leaving Santa Maria della Scala

Map 8.3 - When you exit return to the Cathedral Steps and face away from the steps once more.

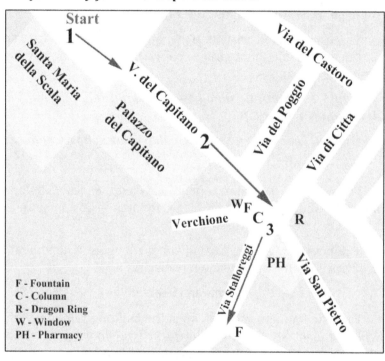

Map 9

Map 9.1 - With the cathedral behind you, turn left to exit the square along Via del Capitano.

The second building you reach on your right is the Palazzo del Capitano. It's made of a lighter stone than its neighbours, and has Sienese arches decorated with porthole windows.

Palazzo del Capitano

This castle-like palace was where Siena's Captain of the People and Captain of War ruled from.

Look up and right at the top you will see many coats of arms running along the façade – those of the families who at some point held office in the building.

There have been various plans and proposals on its sale and development, and perhaps public access. So far nothing has come of them.

Map 9.2 - Continue along Via del Capitano, passing Via del Poggio on your left.

You will reach a little square called Piazza Postierala

Piazza Postierla

You will find a column topped with another She-Wolf and behind it the location of the Eagle fountain – it's sometimes hidden behind parked cars.

The bronze eagle has partially opened wings. The fountain is engraved at the bottom and it translates as:

"Talons and Beaks".

Face the fountain and look up at the building behind it. You will see eight standard windows on two floors, but take a closer look. On the first floor on the left hand side is what is claimed to be the smallest window in the world – complete with louvered shutters.

Farmacia Quattro Cantoni

There is an antique pharmacy on this little square called Farmacia Quattro Cantoni. It dates from at least 1718 and it is possibly older. It's believed it originally served the hospital of

Santa Maria della Scala. Peep inside to see the beautiful decoration.

Now stand with the pharmacy behind you and look diagonally left to see another of Siena's ancient alleyways, Vicolo del Verchione, topped with more medieval arches.

Finally, before you leave the square have a look at the corner of Via di Citti and Via San Pietro to see two ancient rein-rings in the shape of dragons – visitors would tether their horses to the rings. You can spot unusual rein-rings all over Siena so watch out for them.

Map 9.3 - There is another fountain very close by. Stand beside the pharmacy with the she-wolf column and the fountain on your right.

Leave the square by the street straight ahead of you, Via Stalloreggi.

Walk to the next little square, Piazza Conte, to find the Fountain of the Panther.

Fountain of the Panther

It's a very evocative fountain, with the sinuous panther crouching and gazing into the water below it.

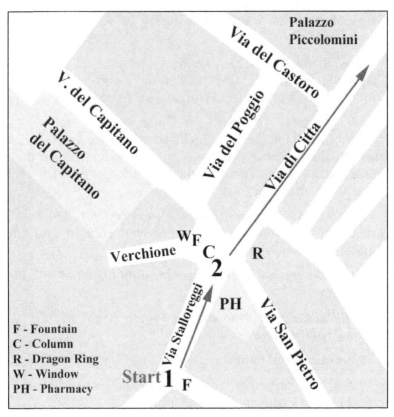

Map 10

Map 10.1 – Backtrack along Via Stalloreggi to return to little Piazza Postierla.

Map 10.2 - Keep straight ahead to walk into Via di Citti.

Keep walking to pass Via del Castoro on your left. The first building on your left, just past Via del Castoro is Palazzo Piccolomini.

Palazzo Piccolomini

It's named after a family you have already met a few times on these walks.

This palace is also known as the Palazzo delle Papesse, as it was originally built by the sister of Pope Pious II, Caterine Piccolomini. The Bank of Italy took it over in 1884 and they restored and renovated it.

In 1998 it was opened to the public as an arts centre, letting the public use the terrace on the second floor and the rooftop terrace, both of which give great views. The Bank's old Strong Room was used as the exhibition space.

It is currently the Salvador Dalí Siena: da Galileo Galilei al Surrealismo – so if you are into surreal art you might want to visit.

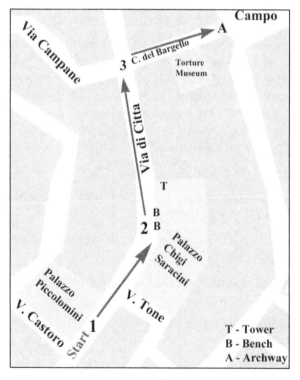

Map 11

Map 11.1 - Continue along Via Citti. As the street curves left you will reach the curved façade of the Palazzo Chigi-Saracini.

Palazzo Chigi-Saracini

There are a couple of stone benches outside the door if you need a sit-down.

This palace has passed through the hands of several of Siena's great families. The builders, the Marescotti family were responsible for the addition of the tower which still stands at the end of the palace. As you know, you are in the Eagle Contrada and if you look up to the first floor you will see an eagle with outstretched wings above each window.

The last owner was Count Chigi Saracini and he added the Music Room, founded a Music Academy, and then bequeathed the building to the Academy. You might hear pianos tinkling as you pass. In the winter months the Academy presents a series of concerts and has being doing so since 1923. The Academy also hosts the Count's art collection with a selection from the best of Siena's artists.

Map 11.2 - Continue along Via di Citti.

Map 11.3 - Take the next right into little Chiasso del Bargello and descend the steps.

You could visit the torture museum which is on your right-hand side at number 6.

Finally pass under an archway and re-enter the Piazza del Campo.

You have now reached the end of this walk.

Walk 4 – Siena South

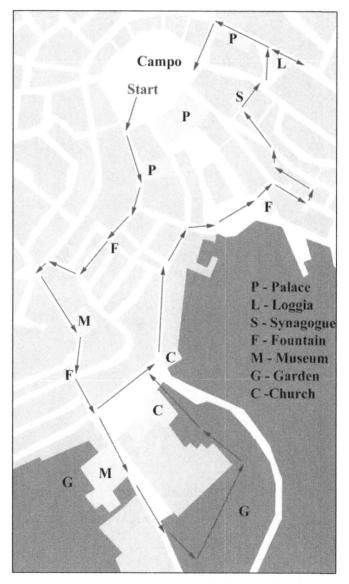

Walk 4 Overview

This walk starts in the Piazza del Campo.

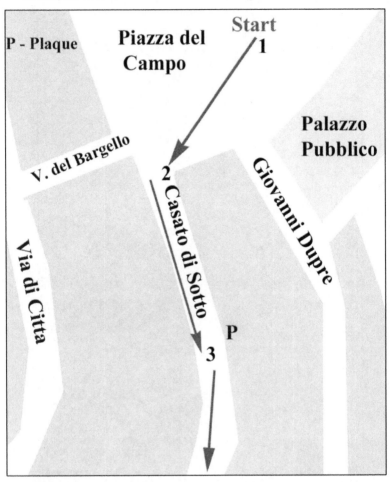

Map 1

Map 1.1 - Face the Palazzo Pubblico. Turn diagonally right and cross the square to the corner.

Map 1.2 - Leave the square by Casato di Sotto.

Casato di Sotto

It's thought that this old street runs along the line of the moat which once guarded Siena. It was later filled with the homes and studios of Siena's merchants and artists.

Fabio Chigi

On your left above the door of number 15 you will see a plaque. It commemorates the palace where Fabio Chigi was born in the seventeenth century. He became Pope Alexander VII.

Map 1.3 - Walk steadily uphill. The road will swing gently to the right.

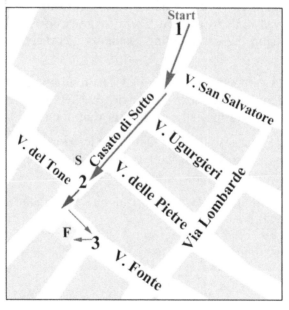

Map 2

Map 2.1 - Pass Vicolo San Salvatore, Vicolo Ugurgieri, and Vicolo delle Pietre which are all on your left-hand side.

Pause at the corner of Vicolo del Tone on your right.

There is a little shrine at the corner.   Every year the children of the Eagle contrada parade around the streets, and they lay flowers at this little shrine with its image of the Virgin Mary.

Map 2.2 - Continue along Casato di Sotto a few more steps to reach Vicolo Fonte on your left. You will find a narrow stairway to descend by, so pop downstairs

Map 2.3 - At the bottom of the steps turn right to find a further flight of stairs which will take you down to see another fountain, the Fonte del Casato.

Fonte del Casato

This fountain is not owned by any Contrada but it is very old. It was built in the fourteenth century in response to a petition from the surrounding residents who needed a water source.

As you can see it's not the easiest fountain to reach, and going up and down those steps with buckets of water seems positively dangerous - so it was never that popular.

When Siena was finally taken over by Florence, an official was sent to record important structures including fountains, and this one was just forgotten about.

The fountain was walled up at one point and was only rescued in the 1970s.

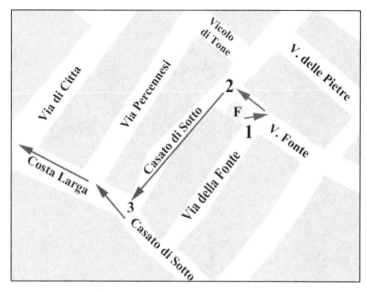

Map 3

Map 3.1 - Return back up both sets of stairs to Casato di Sotto.

Map 3.2 - Turn left along Casato di Sotto.   You will reach a junction with Costa Larga on the right and Casato di Sotto continuing on the left.

Map 3.3 - Turn right into Costa Largo.

Pass Via Percennesi on the right and you will reach a T-junction with Via di Citti once more.

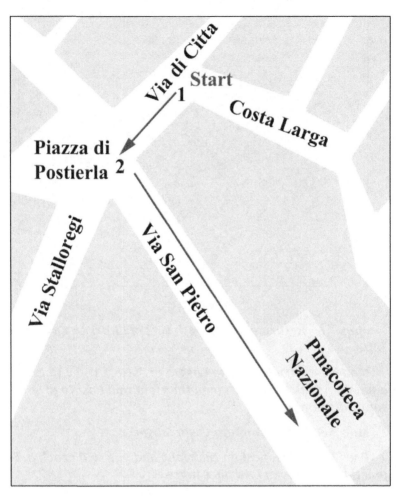

Map 4

Map 4.1 - Turn left along Via di Citti to reach Piazza di Postierla. You may recognise this square from Walk 3.

Map 4.2 - Turn left to go down Via San Pietro. When you reach number 40 on your right you will find the Pinacoteca Nazionale on your left.

If you are fond of golden gothic paintings then this huge collection is for you. If you are not interested, press on to "Leaving the Pinacoteca Nazionale" on Page 141.

Pinacoteca Nazionale

If you go into the museum you will first enter a pleasant courtyard. Inside, the museum holds some of the masterpieces by the best of Sienese artists. Try to find the following highlights:

The Adoration of the Magi - Bartolo di Fredi

Fredi was a very successful Sienese painter who produced many altarpieces and frescoes. This work is from one of his altarpieces of which three panels survive. The other two are in Virginia USA, and Germany.

This painting is not only good to look at, but shows the transition from the stiff inanimate gothic style so loved by Siena to a more dynamic animated Renaissance style. The kings all seem to be in motion and even the horses seem lively.

In the background stands Siena's cathedral dressed in its black and white marble.

Saint Anthony beaten by devils – Sassetta

This is part of an altarpiece which was commissioned by the very wealthy Wool Merchants Guild, which was also later split up.

Saint Anthony was both tortured and tempted by devils to test his faith – and here we see one of the more unpleasant tests.

The Virgin appears to Pope Callistus - Sano di Pietro

This apparently shows the Virgin Mary asking the Pope to aid the people of Siena as the Black Death wipes out most of the population, however it does look as though she is giving him a telling-off.

At the bottom of the picture you can see mules carrying sacks of grain into the desperate city. You can make out the Tower of the Palazzo Pubblico and the Cathedral.

The Stigmata of Santa Caterina of Siena- Domenico Beccafumi

Here you see Santa Caterina receiving her stigmata, an event which you might have read about on Walk 3.

Nativity of the Virgin - Domenico Beccafumi

This baby in the painting of course is the Virgin Mary, but what makes the painting stand out are the oddly long thin fingers of the women in the room, especially the lady on the right.

Agostino Novello and Four of his Miracles – Simone Martini

Saint Agostino died in 1309 and was so highly regarded that he was made a saint almost immediately. This glowing painting was commissioned in his honour in 1320.

It shows us four of his miracles, which seem to involve a lot of people falling down and having to be brought back to life:

The child attacked by a wolf
The knight and his horse that fell down a ravine
The boy who fell from a balcony
The child who fell from a cradle

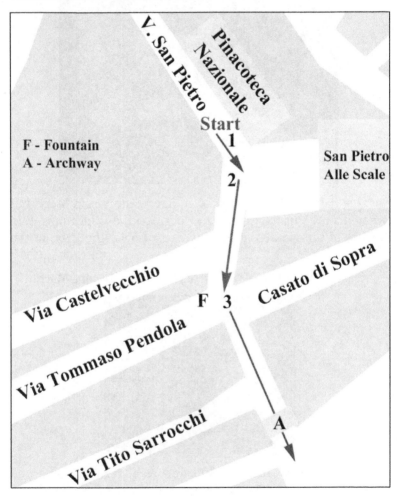

Map 5

Leaving the Pinacoteca Nazionale

Map 5.1 - With the museum door behind you, turn left along Via San Pietro. You will pass San Pietro Alle Scale, which sits at the top of some steps on your left.

San Pietro Alle Scale

It's one of the oldest churches in the city although it's been renovated a couple of times. Above the door is Saint Peter holding his keys.

Map 5.2 – Continue along Via San Peitro passing Via Castelvecchio on your right. You are now entering the Contrada of the Turtle.

It is the oldest Contrada and traditionally the residents were sculptors. Their motto is:

Power and Consistency

Map 5.3 - Keep walking straight ahead and just a few more steps will bring you to a crossroads with Casato di Spora and Via Tommaso Pendola.

The turtle fountain is on your right hand-side in Via Tommaso Pendola.

Contrada of the Turtle

The contrada fountain is a pretty affair, with a turtle and a little boy climbing on board or a ride. .

The Contrada of the Turtle was the first to commission a bespoke fountain, however when the fountain was presented to the contrada they were not impressed. So a second fountain was commissioned – but by a different sculptor! This one got the nod of approval.

Map 5.3 - Continue along Via San Pietro and walk through the Porta all'Arco.

Porta all'Arco

The gate which you just passed through is first mentioned in the history books in the thirteenth century. It was part of the city wall from that period. The gate itself is long gone and we are left with only the archway.

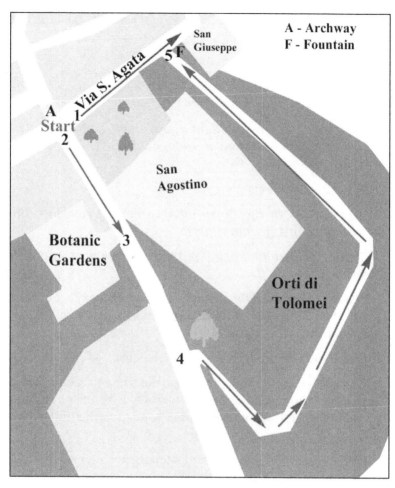

Map 6

In front of you, you will see a sizeable square. On it behind the trees stands the church of San Agostino which is now used for concerts.

You have a choice now. You could take a walk around the botanical gardens and a park which gives you some nice views over Tuscany. Or you can skip those and just take the quickest route to the next Contrada.

To the Next Contrada

Map 6.1 - With the Porta all'Arco behind you, face the square and San Agostino church.

Turn left along Via Sant'Agata and walk downhill towards the San Giuseppe church. Continue the walk from San Giuseppe on Page 145.

Flowers and Views

Map 6.2 - With the Porta all'Arco behind you, face the square and San Agostino church.

Continue straight ahead passing the square and San Agostino on your left.

You will find the Botanical Gardens entrance on your right - you can spot shrubs and palm trees through the metal fence.

Botanical Gardens

The garden was originally sited next to the Santa Maria della Scala hospital and was used to grow medicinal plants, but it was moved to this location and expanded in the nineteenth century.

If you venture in you will find silence except perhaps from the buzz of insects in summer.

Some of the plants grown are fascinating; for example there is the albero dei rosari whose beans have a little hole in place which makes them perfect for rosary beads.

The gardens are supposedly haunted! The ghost was first seen in the 1930's and investigators have decided he is Brother Giacomo dè Magagni who was hung for having an affair with a nun in the sixteenth century. It's not explained why he took 300 years to start making appearances. He has been sighted at the front gate and there are even reports of the good Friar throwing rocks at passers-by. It adds a little spice to your visit – especially if you are visiting near dusk.

Map 6.3 - When you exit, continue downhill.

The buildings on your right are part of the University.

As the road bends a bit to the right, you will see another of Siena's old gates at the bottom of the hill. However don't go that far.

Instead go through a gap in the wall on the left-hand side into Orti di Tolomei! The gap is under a large over-hanging tree.

Orti di Tolomei

There is a pleasant track around this garden which will give you good views over the Tuscan countryside. Perhaps stopping to sit down and relax for a while.

Map 6.4 - Follow the path as it turns left and eventually you will climb up the hill once more.

Exit the park at the back of Santa Agnostino.

Map 6.5 - The church of San Giuseppe is on your right, so walk down towards it.

San Giuseppe

This is the church of Contrada of the Wave. When Siena was an independent republic, the people from this Contrada were responsible for the shore defences on the Tyrrhenian Sea. Their pretty dolphin fountain is just next to the church.

The Contrada holds a festival each March in front of the church and in the surrounding streets. The church is dressed in green garlands, flowers, and banners decorated with dolphins. Stalls are set up here and in the Campo selling Frittelle di San Giuseppe – little rice balls.

The Contrada museum is in the crypt of the church, and the Victory Room proudly displays the Palio banners won by the Contrada. Their motto is:

The colour of the sky, the power of the ocean

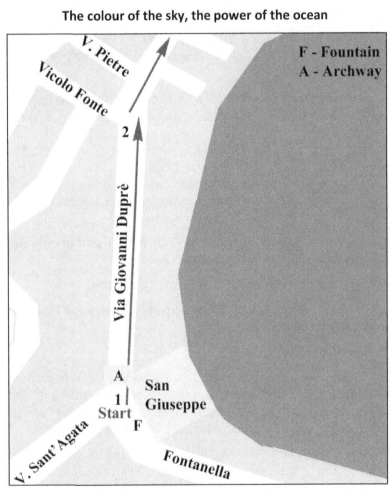

Map 7

Map 7.1 - With the church door behind you, turn right to go through the archway.

Movie note - James Bond also goes through this archway in his Aston Martin in Quantum of Solace.

Walk downhill on Via Giovanni Dupre.

Giovanni Dupre

This street is named after one of Siena's most famous sculptors. His works can be found in the Uffizi Museum in Florence, and in the Hermitage Museum in St Petersburg. His greatest piece is thought to be a Pieta (Mary holding the body of Christ) which is in Fiesole.

The Wave Contrade is so proud of him that he is mentioned in one of the verses of their anthem:

> The greatest patron watches over you,
> Siena is honored in the world for you
> of Duprè who falls in love with faith
> with the beautiful immortal "Pietà

Map 7.2 - As the street bends right, pass Vicolo Fonte and Vicolo delle Pietre on your left.

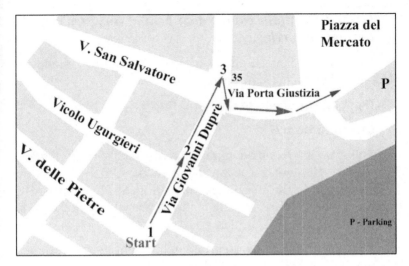

Map 8

Map 8.1 – Keep walking downhill, passing Vicolo Ugurgieri on your left.

Map 8.2 – You will next reach a crossroads with Via Porta Giustizia on your right and Via San Salvatore on your left.

Take a few steps beyond the crossroads to the house on your right, marked as number 35.

Giovanni Dupre Again

There is a plaque on the house, as that is where Giovanni was born. It translates as:

This humble house where Giovanni Dupré was born,
an honour of art and of Italy,
reminds the children of the people
that the power of genius and will can succeed.

Map 8.3 - Now backtrack a few steps to the crossroads again. Go downhill on Via Porta Giustizia which is now on your left.

You will soon walk into the old market square, Piazza del Mercato.

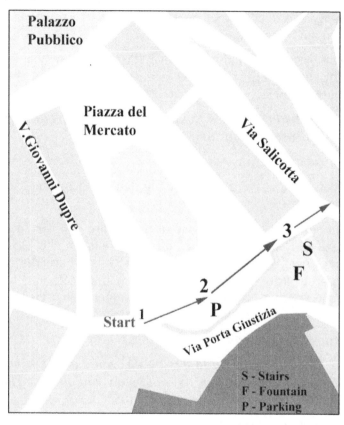

Map 9

Piazza Del Mercato

Sadly the market square is now more or less a car park but it used to be full of trees, and it was where cattle, flowers vegetables etc. were traded.

Map 9.1 – You will see Via Porta Giustizia dropping away to your right.

Death March

Siena's prison stood not too far away, and criminals sentenced to death would be taken from there to the Piazza Mercato in wagons.

The wagons would then leave the square by Via Porta Giustiza and exit the city by the Justice Gate. Outside that gate stood the gallows.

Walk straight across the elevated area in front of you. It's mostly used for parking.

Pause halfway across the square.

Look over to your right for another view of the Tuscan countryside.

On your left on the far side of the square you can see the Palazzo Pubblico. There are often tourists on the balcony gazing down at the view. That balcony is where the Nine would retreat to, perhaps to look at the view, get some fresh air and refresh themselves – remember they were not permitted to exit the Palazzo.

Map 9.2 - Continue straight across the square.

As you approach buildings again, you can see a small building with openings in its roof below you on your right-hand side. That is the Market Fountain.

Market Fountain

It was used right up to the mid-twentieth century as a watering place for the animals brought to market.

It's not open, but if you are curious you could walk down the stairs a little further along on the right. Peep through the railings for a closer look.

If you have climbed down for a look at the fountain, make your way back up the steps.

Map 9.3 – With the fountain and steps on your right-hand side, continue straight ahead. Leave the piazza by Via Malcontenti to reach a T-junction with Via Salicotta.

Via Salicotta was where Siena's prison once stood.

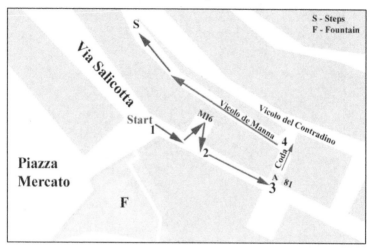

Map 10

Map 10.1 - Turn right, and you will find tiny Piazzetta Della Paglietta almost immediately on your left.

James Bond

This little square was used in the James Bond film Quantum of Solace. Bond arrives in his Aston Martin and enters the "MI6 safe house" through the double doors you see in front of you.

Map 10.2 - Continue along Via Salicotto but watch out for an archway on the left – it's just before number 81.

Map 10.3 - Go through the archway and up Vicolo della Coda.

Map 10.4 - You will reach Vicolo de Manna, where you turn left to walk along with a wall on your right. This street will then narrow and a set of stairs will take you up.

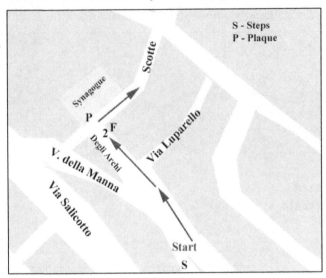

Map 11

Map 11.1 - Just ahead of you is a fork. Take the right hand street, passing Via Luparello on your right. Walk straight into Via Degli Archi.

The Ghetto

This takes you into the old Ghetto area. At the end of the street you will find the synagogue which you could visit to see the rich interior.

Sienna's Jewish citizens had mixed fortunes over the centuries. The Jews were blamed for the plague when it arrived and were forced to live outside the city walls.

Life improved after the plague; they were given complete religious freedom, allowed to live and work in the city, and even attend the University. However it got worse again in

152

1555 - they had to live in the Ghetto, wear yellow caps and scarves, and pay a special tax.

Things improved again in the eighteenth century. They were given complete freedom by Napoleon's army in March 1799, only for rioters to wreak havoc and murder the Jews in June of the same year.

The Jewish population then started to leave Siena en masse.

The ghetto existed until 1859, but all that remains now are some street signs. We all know what happened to the Jews in WWII, and afterwards only about one hundred Jews remained in Sienna.

The two plaques next to the Synagogue door commemorate the Jews who were deported in WWII, and the Jews who were burned alive during the riots in 1799.

Before leaving this sad area, face the synagogue door and turn right to find the Fonte del Ghetto.

Fonte del Ghetto

The Ghetto was packed with families so a fountain was a necessity. It used to be decorated with a statue of Moses hitting a rock with a stick to make the water flow out.

That statue is now in the Municipal Museum, but it would be nice if even just a copy could be reinstalled in the fountain.

Map 11.2 - Face the fountain. Leave by continuing through tiny Vicolo delle Scotte which you will find just to the left of the fountain.

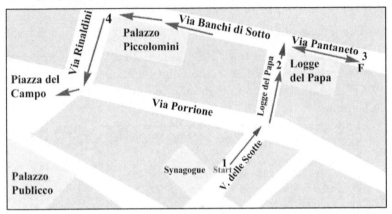

Map 12

Map 12.1 – At the end of the street you will reach a crossroads with Via Porrione. Cross over Via Porrione and into Logge del Papa.

Walk straight ahead to reach the columned Logge del Papa building on your right.

Logge del Papa

It was built by Pope Pious II for the fame of his family, the Piccolominis. Above the arches of the Logge you can read:

PIUS II PONT MAX GENTILIBVS SVIS PICCOLOMINEIS

Pius II Pontifex Maximus to his Piccolomini relatives

The Piccolominis became very rich when they became the Papal bankers – it's always useful to have a family member in a powerful position! It was Pope Pious II who built the

154

Piccolomini library you might have already seen in the cathedral on walk 3.

Map 12.2 - Continue to the end of the street to reach a T-junction with Via Pantaneto.

Take a little diversion by turning right into Via Pantaneto. Just a few steps along on the right is another fountain, the La Fonte di Pantaneto

La Fonte di Pantaneto

It was added in the fifteenth century, again as a result of a petition from thirsty locals. It was adopted by the Unicorn Contrada, - the twin unicorn heads were added in 1887 to make the baptisms a bit more special.

Map 12.3 - Backtrack along Via Pantaneto to the Logge del Papa once more, and continue straight ahead onto Via Banchi di Sotto. On your left you will find the beautiful Palazzo Piccolomini on your left.

Palazzo Piccolomini

You can see the coat of arms of the Piccolomini family on the front façade above the main door. It was built by Giacomo and Andrea Piccolomini, who were nephews of Pope Pious II.

The last member of the family died in the seventeenth century, and the palace was rented by the Collegio Tolomei, a college for the sons of the well-off.

When the college left, the palace was taken over by the city administration and now houses the State Archive. It's free to wander around so pop in. It's quite opulent and has a pretty courtyard.

Map 12.4 – When you exit, turn left into Banchi di Sotto. Take the first left left into Via Rinaldini, to reach the Campo and perhaps a well-earned coffee in one of the many cafes.

Did you enjoy these walks?

I do hope you found the walks both fun and interesting, and I would love feedback. If you have any comments, either good or bad, please review this book

You could also drop me a line on my amazon web page.

Other Strolling Around Books to try:

- Strolling Around Bilbao
- Strolling Around Arles
- Strolling Around Bruges
- Strolling Around Jerez
- Strolling Around Verona
- Strolling Around Palma
- Strolling Around Ljubljana
- Strolling Around Berlin
- Strolling Around The Hague
- Strolling Around Porto
- Strolling Around Lucca
- Strolling Around Amsterdam
- Strolling Around Madrid
- Strolling Around Lisbon
- Strolling Around Ghent
- Strolling Around Delft
- Strolling Around Florence
- Strolling Around Toledo
- Strolling Around Bath
- Strolling Around Antwerp
- Strolling Around Pisa

Printed by Amazon Italia Logistica S.r.l.
Torrazza Piemonte (TO), Italy

47844731R00090